Third Edition

THE
NEW YORK
NOTARY LAW
PRIMER

*All the hard-to-find information
every New York Notary Public
needs to know!*

National Notary Association
A Nonprofit Educational Organization

Published by:
National Notary Association
A Nonprofit Educational Organization
9350 De Soto Ave., P.O. Box 2402
Chatsworth, CA 91313-2402
Telephone: 1-818-739-4000
FAX: 1-818-700-0920
Web site: www.nationalnotary.org
E-mail: nna@nationalnotary.org

Third Edition © 1997
First Edition © 1987

Library of Congress Catalog Card No. 87-61369
ISBN No. 0-933134-88-6

Table
of Contents

Introduction

You are to be commended on your interest in New York Notary law! Purchasing *The New York Notary Law Primer* identifies you as a conscientious professional who takes your official responsibilities seriously.

In few fields is the expression "more to it than meets the eye" truer than in Notary law. What often appears on the surface to be a simple procedure may, in fact, have important legal considerations.

The purpose of *The New York Notary Law Primer* is to provide you with a resource to help you decipher the many intricate laws that affect notarization. In doing so, the *Primer* will acquaint you with all important aspects of New York's Notary law and with prudent notarial practices in general.

This 1997 edition of *The New York Notary Law Primer* has been updated to include all recent pertinent law changes.

While *The New York Notary Law Primer* begins with informative chapters on how to obtain your commission, what tools the Notary needs, often-asked questions and critical steps in notarization, the heart of this book is the chapter entitled "Notary Laws Explained." Here, we take you through the myriad of Notary laws and put them in easy-to-understand terms. Every section of the law is analyzed and explained, as well as topics not covered by New York law but nonetheless of vital concern to you as a Notary.

For handy reference, we have reprinted the *Notary Public License Law* (NPLL), the New York Department of State's compilation of laws relating to Notaries Public. In addition, we have included addresses and phone numbers of Department of State offices, County Clerk offices, Bureaus of Vital Statistics, plus a list of nations that are parties to the Hague Convention, a treaty which simplifies the process of authentication.

Whether you're about to be commissioned for the first time or a longtime Notary, we're sure *The New York Notary Law Primer* will provide you with new insights and understanding. Your improved comprehension of New York's Notary law will naturally result in your greater competence as a professional Notary Public.

Milton G. Valera
President
National Notary Association

How to Become a New York Notary Public

1. Ensure that you comply with the basic qualifications for a New York Notary commission.

You must meet the basic requirements to become a Notary in the state of New York. First, you must be 18 years of age or older. Second, you must be a New York resident or maintain a business or office in the state. And third, you must not have been convicted of a felony.

Although the New York Executive Law, Section 130, states that an applicant must be a U.S. citizen, a 1984 U.S. Supreme Court decision, *Bernal v. Fainter*, declared that no state may deny a Notary commission merely on the basis of lack of U.S. citizenship.

2. Obtain a commission application and Notary exam study materials.

If you are applying for a Notary commission for the first time, you must pass a written and proctored examination administered at designated sites throughout New York.

Notaries seeking to renew their commissions and former New York Notaries whose commissions have been expired less than six months are exempt from taking the exam. However, an application for reappointment is still required.

To receive a commission application and study materials (the *Notary Public License Law*) for the exam, call the Department of State at 1-518-474-4429, 9:00 a.m. to 4:45 p.m., Monday through Friday (applicants with touch-tone phones may call 24 hours a day). Your request for the application and study materials may also be faxed to the Department at 1-518-473-6648. Include your name and address, as well as the type and quantity of forms

3

desired. (Specify whether you just want an application or a complete package, which includes the application, study materials and examination schedule. One applicant may request more than one application or complete package.) The application is also available at Department of State offices in Albany, Binghamton, Buffalo, Hauppuage, New York City, Syracuse and Utica. Depending on supply, the application may be available at County Clerk offices. See page 105 for addresses of these offices.

3. Study the *Notary Public License Law.*

The 40-question, multiple-choice exam is based on the *Notary Public License Law,* which should be studied thoroughly. It is also helpful to review the "Notary Laws Explained" chapter of this *Primer,* starting on page 17.

4. Complete the application.

Follow the clear instructions on the reverse side of the application and complete the application in ink. On the application, you may not use a post office box as an address. In addition, a married woman must use her own name, not that of her spouse (for example, "Jane Smith," not "Mrs. John Smith"). Sign and date the form.

Any false statements or omission of any information required by this form is cause for denial of a Notary commission.

Take the completed application form to a commissioned Notary Public who will give you the required oath of office. You will mail the notarized application along with your exam slip after you take and pass the exam.

Notaries seeking reappointment must submit their applications to the local County Clerk, not the Department of State. The application may be picked up at the County Clerk's office or at any office of the Department of State, or call 1-518-474-4429 to have one mailed to you. The application must be completed in ink and its oath of office portion notarized. Submit the application and a nonrefundable fee of $30 to the County Clerk. All business regarding renewing Notaries should be directed to the County Clerk's office.

5. Find the next available exam in your area.

Determine a convenient site and time for the exam by calling the Department of State at 1-518-474-4429.

Exams are given regularly in the following cities: Albany,

Binghamton, Buffalo, Elmsford, Franklin Square, Hauppuage, Newburgh, New York City, Plattsburgh, Rochester, Syracuse, Utica and Watertown. Exams are administered at state office buildings and other state-designated sites.

6. Take the exam.

Since there is no preregistration or guarantee of space, applicants must report to the selected site at least 15 minutes before the scheduled starting time of the exam. The policy is first-come, first-served.

Be prepared to present photo identification (a valid New York driver's license, a nondriver ID or a current passport); commission fees ($15 for first-time applicants, payable to "Department of State" by check or money order — cash will not be accepted); two sharp #2 black lead pencils; and thumbprints (applicants are required to provide a thumbprint at the time of the exam). Any applicants who have been designated by a County Clerk to serve the public at no charge are exempted from the fee.

You will be given 60 minutes to complete the exam. At least 70 percent of the questions must be answered correctly to pass. Study and reference materials may not be used during the test.

7. File your exam results, application and oath of office.

Within approximately 10 business days after taking the exam, you will be informed by mail whether you passed or failed. Scores will not be released or discussed over the telephone. If you pass the exam, return your original exam slip (not a photocopy) marked "Passed," along with your application, a signed and notarized oath of office and an application fee of $30 within two years to: Department of State, Division of Licensing Services, 84 Holland Ave., Albany, NY 12208-3490. Failure to file within two years will invalidate the results of the exam. If you fail — your exam slip will be marked "Failed" — you may take the exam again at any time.

If your application is approved, the Department of State will send you an identification card stating the effective and expiration dates of your two-year commission. The Department will send your Notary commission directly to the local County Clerk, along with a copy of your oath of office and official signature to keep on file. The Notary does not have to appear at a county office to pick up the commission; it remains on file with the County Clerk. The Notary retains only the Department-issued Notary identification card. ■

Tools of the Trade

There are several tools that Notaries need to carry out their duties lawfully and efficiently. These tools are as important to the Notary as a hammer and saw are to the carpenter.

Inking Stamp

Although not required by New York law, an inked stamp may be convenient to imprint certain required data on the document. The following information must be typed, printed or stamped on each notarial certificate: the Notary's name, the words "Notary Public State of New York," the name of the county where the Notary originally qualified, the Notary's commission expiration date, and the name of the county in which the Notary's certificate of official character may be filed, using the words "Certificate filed _____ County."

Seal Embosser

While not required by New York law, the seal embosser is used in many states and is often vital on documents sent abroad. Many New York Notaries opt to affix an embossment in addition to an inked stamp. The seal embosser makes a nonphotographically reproducible indentation on the document. Because photocopies of documents can easily pass as originals, the embossment can be used to distinguish an original from a photocopy. Also, embossing all pages in a document together can safeguard against later substitution or addition of pages.

Journal of Notarial Acts

New York law does not require Notaries to keep journals, but many lawsuits may be prevented when Notaries can demonstrate, through a detailed and accurate journal record, that they have exercised reasonable care in executing their notarial acts. The journal should include the date, time, and type of each official act; the type of document notarized; the signature of each person whose signature is notarized; the method used to identify the signers; and the fee charged.

Jurat Stamp

The jurat stamp impresses on an affidavit the jurat wording "Subscribed and sworn to before me this _____ day of _____, _____, by _____." More convenient than typing the wording on each affidavit that requires it (and safer, since critical wording will not be omitted), the jurat stamp is both handy and practical.

Venue Stamp

The venue stamp is used in conjunction with the jurat stamp in a jurat. The phrase, "State of _____, County of _____," indicates where the jurat was executed. Also usable for acknowledgments.

Thumbprinting Device

Increasingly, Notaries are requiring signers to affix a thumbprint in the journal. A thumbprint serves as proof that a particular signer did or did not appear, thereby deterring forgers. Many Notaries opt for the convenience of an inexpensive single-digit fingerprinting device.

Notarial Certificates

Preprinted notarial certificates for acknowledgments, jurats, proofs of execution by a subscribing witness, and for copy certification by a document custodian are available and convenient to have on hand.

Errors and Omissions Insurance

Notary errors and omissions insurance provides protection for Notaries who are sued for damages resulting from unintentional notarial mistakes. In the event of a lawsuit, the "E&O" insurance company will provide and pay for the Notary's legal counsel and absorb any damages levied by a court or agreed to in a settlement, up to the coverage limit. Errors and omissions insurance does not cover the Notary for intentional misconduct. ■

As a full-service organization, the National Notary Association makes available to New York Notaries all notarial items required by law, custom and convenience.

10 Most-Asked Questions

Every Notary has a question or two about whether and how to notarize. But there are certain questions that pop up again and again. These top 10 questions are asked repeatedly at the National Notary Association's seminars, its annual National Conference of Notaries Public and through its *Notary Information Service*.

As with most questions about notarization, the answer to these 10 is not always a simple "yes" or "no." Rather, the answer is, "It depends...."

Here's what every Notary wants to know:

1. Can I notarize a will?

Sometimes. A Notary should only notarize a document described as a will if clear instructions and a notarial certificate are provided. If the signer of the will is relying on the Notary for advice on how to proceed, the Notary should refer the individual to an attorney.

Laws regarding wills differ from state to state. Some states do not require notarization of wills, while others allow it as one of several witnessing options. Usually, it is not the will itself that is notarized, but accompanying affidavits signed by witnesses.

The danger in notarizing wills is that would-be testators who have drafted their own wills without legal advice may believe that notarization will make their wills legal and valid. However, even when notarized, such homemade wills may be worthless because the testators failed to obtain the proper number of witnesses or omitted important information.

In fact, notarization itself may actually void an otherwise properly executed handwritten (holographic) will, because courts have occasionally held that any writing on the document other than the testator's could invalidate the will. In New York, the signatures of the witnesses may be notarized on a self-proving will.

2. Can I notarize for a stranger with no identification?

Yes. If identification of a signer cannot be based on personal knowledge or identification documents (ID cards), a Notary may rely on the oath or affirmation of a personally known credible witness to identify an unknown signer.

If a credible witness is used, the Notary must personally know the credible witness, who must personally know the document signer. This establishes a chain of personal knowledge from the Notary to the credible witness to the signer.

A credible witness should be someone the Notary believes to be trustworthy and impartial. If a person has a financial or other beneficial interest in a document, that individual could not be a reliable witness.

When no credible witness is available to identify a stranger without IDs, the Notary may have no choice but to tell the signer to find a personally known Notary or a friend who personally knows a Notary, if the signer is unable to obtain an adequate identification document.

3. Can I notarize a photograph?

No. To simply stamp and sign a photograph is improper. A Notary's signature and seal must appear only on a notarial certificate (such as an acknowledgment or jurat) accompanying a written statement signed by another person.

However, a signature on a written statement referring to an accompanying or attached photograph may be notarized; if the photograph is large enough, the statement and notarial certificate might even appear on its reverse side. Such a format may be acceptable when notarized photos are requested by persons seeking medical or health licenses, or by legal resident aliens renewing foreign passports.

A word of caution here: a Notary should always be suspicious about notarizing a photo-bearing card or document that could be used as a bogus "official" ID.

4. What if there's no room for my seal or if it smears?

Usually, if notarial wording printed on a document leaves no room for a seal, a loose certificate can be attached and filled out instead, provided the certificate wording is substantially the same as on the document.

If an initial seal impression is unreadable and there is ample room on the document, another impression can be affixed nearby. The illegibility of the first impression will indicate why a second seal impression was necessary. And the Notary should record in the journal that a second seal was applied.

A Notary should *never* attempt to fix an imperfect seal impression with pen and ink. This may be viewed as evidence of tampering and could cause the document's rejection by a recorder.

5. Can I notarize signatures on photocopies of documents?

Yes. A photocopy may be notarized as long as it bears an *original* signature. That is, the photocopy must have been signed with pen and ink. A photocopied signature may *never* be notarized.

Note that some public recorders will not accept notarized signatures on photocopied sheets because they will not adequately reproduce in microfilming.

When carbon copies are made, the Notary will sometimes be asked to conform rather than to notarize the copies. To conform a copy, the Notary affixes the official seal on the copy (carbon will not readily transfer a seal impression) and writes "conformed copy" prominently across the top of the copy.

6. Can I notarize for customers only?

No. As a public official, a Notary is not commissioned to serve just the customers or clients of any one business, even when the employer has paid for the bond, commissioning fees and notarial supplies. There is no such officer as a "Notary Private."

It is ethically improper — although hardly ever explicitly prohibited by statute — to discriminate between customers and noncustomers in offering or refusing to offer notarial services and in charging or not charging fees.

Discrimination against anyone who presents a lawful request for notarization is not a suitable policy for a public official commissioned to serve all of the public equally. Also, such discrimination can provide the basis for lawsuits.

7. Can I notarize a document in a language I can't read?

Yes. As long as the notarial certificate and document signature are in a language the Notary *can* read, New York Notaries are not expressly prohibited from notarizing documents written in languages they *cannot* read.

However, there are certain difficulties and dangers in notarizing documents that the Notary cannot read. The main difficulty for the Notary is making an accurate journal description of an unreadable document; the main danger is that the document may be blatantly fraudulent.

Under no circumstances should a notarization be performed if the Notary and the principal signer cannot communicate in the same language.

8. Can I certify a copy of a birth certificate?

No. Some states — although not New York — do allow Notaries to certify copies, but copies of documents that are either public records or publicly recordable should never be certified by Notaries. Only an officer in a bureau of vital statistics should certify a copy of a birth certificate or other vital public record. A Notary's "certification" of a birth or death record may actually lend credibility to a counterfeit or tampered document. Only a county recording official should certify a copy of a deed or other recordable instrument.

In states allowing Notary-certified copies, the types of documents of which Notaries may properly certify copies are original personal papers, such as letters and college diplomas, and in-house business documents.

9. Does a document have to be signed in my presence?

No and yes. Documents requiring acknowledgments normally do not need to be signed in the Notary's presence. However, the signer *must* appear before the Notary at the time of notarization to acknowledge that he or she freely signed for the purposes stated in the document.

An acknowledgment certificate indicates that the signer personally appeared before the Notary, was identified by the Notary, and acknowledged to the Notary that the document was freely signed.

On the other hand, documents requiring a jurat typically *must* be signed in the Notary's presence, as dictated by the typical

jurat wording, "Subscribed (signed) and sworn to before me..."
However, if a jurat merely reads "Sworn to before me...," then
the signature need not be affixed in the Notary's presence.

In executing a jurat, a Notary guarantees that the signer:
personally appeared before the Notary, was given an oath or
affirmation by the Notary, and, usually, signed in the Notary's
presence. In addition, even though it may not be a statutory
requirement that the Notary positively identify a signer for a
jurat, it is always a good idea to do so.

10. Can I notarize for a family member?

Yes and no. Although state law does not prohibit notarizing
for family members, Notaries who do so may violate the statutes
prohibiting a direct beneficial interest — especially in notarizing
for spouses in states with community property laws.

Besides the possibility of a financial interest in notarizing for
a relative, there may be an "emotional interest" that can prevent
the Notary from acting impartially. For example, a Notary who is
asked to notarize a contract signed by his brother might attempt
to persuade the sibling to sign or not sign. As a brother, the
individual is entitled to exert influence — but this is entirely
improper for a Notary.

Even if a Notary has no direct beneficial interest in the
document and does not attempt to influence the signer,
notarizing for a relative could subject the document to a legal
challenge if other parties to the transaction allege that the Notary
could not have acted impartially. ■

Steps to Proper Notarization

What constitutes reasonable care?

If a Notary can convincingly show that he or she used every reasonable precaution expected of a person of ordinary prudence and intelligence, then the Notary has exercised reasonable care — a shield against liability.

The following 14-step checklist will help Notaries apply reasonable care and avert the most common pitfalls.

1. Require every signer to personally appear.

The signer *must* appear in person before the Notary on the date and in the county stated in the notarial certificate. "Personal appearance" means the signer is in the Notary's physical presence — face to face in the same room. A telephone call is not acceptable as personal appearance.

2. Make a careful identification.

The Notary should identify every document signer through either personal knowledge, the word of a credible witness under oath, or through reliable identification documents (ID cards).

When using ID cards, the Notary must examine them closely to detect alteration, counterfeiting or evidence that they are issued to an impostor. Don't rely on a type of card with which you are unfamiliar, unless you check it against a reference such as the *U.S. Identification Manual* or the *ID Checking Guide*.

3. Feel certain the signer is competent.

A conscientious and careful Notary will be certain not only of the signer's identity and willingness to sign, but also will make a layperson's judgment about the signer's ability to understand the document. This ability to understand is called competence.

A document signer who cannot respond intelligibly in a simple conversation with the Notary should not be considered competent to sign at that moment. If in doubt, the Notary might ask the signer if he or she understands the document and can explain its purpose. Or, if in a medical environment, the signer's doctor can be consulted for a professional opinion.

4. Check the signature.

The Notary *must* make sure that the document signer signs the same name appearing on the identification presented.

To check for possible forgery, the Notary should compare the signature that the person leaves in the journal of notarial acts against the signatures on the document and on the IDs. Also, it should be noted whether the signer appears to be laboring on the journal signature, a possible indication of forgery in progress.

In certain circumstances, it may be acceptable for a signer to sign with an abbreviated form of his or her name (John D. Smith instead of John David Smith, for example), as long as the individual is signing with *less* than and not *more* than what is on the identification document.

5. Look for blank spaces.

Documents with blank spaces have a great potential for fraudulent misuse. A borrower, for example, might sign an incomplete promissory note, trusting the lender to fill it out, and then later find that the lender has written in an amount in excess of what was actually borrowed.

If the blanks are inapplicable and intended to be left unfilled, the signer should be asked to line through each space (using ink), or to write in "Not Applicable" or "NA."

6. Scan the document.

Notaries are not required to read the documents they notarize. However, they should note certain important particulars about a document, such as its title, for recording in the journal of notarial acts. Notaries must be sure to count and record the number of pages; this can show whether pages are later fraudulently added or removed.

7. Check the document's date.

For acknowledgments, the date of signing on the document

must either precede or be the same as the date of the notarization, but not follow it. For a jurat, the document signing date and the notarization date are typically the same.

A document dated after the date on its notarial certificate risks rejection by a recorder, who may question how the document could have been notarized before it was signed.

8. Keep a journal of notarial acts.

Although not required by New York State law, a journal is recommended for all Notaries. If a notarized document is lost or altered, or if certain facts about the transaction are later challenged, the Notary's journal becomes valuable evidence. It can protect the rights of all parties to a transaction and help Notaries defend themselves against false accusations.

The Notary should include *all* the pertinent details of the notarization in the journal, such as the date, time and type of notarization, the date and type of document, the signature, printed name and address of the signer, how this person was identified and notarial fees charged, if any. Any other pertinent data, such as the capacity the signer is claiming, may also be entered.

9. Complete the journal entry first.

The Notary should complete the journal entry entirely *before* filling out the notarial certificate. This prevents a signer from leaving before the important public record of the notarization is made in the journal.

10. Make sure the document has notarial wording.

If a notarial certificate does not come with the document, the Notary must ask the document signer what type of notarization — acknowledgment or jurat — is required. The Notary may then type the appropriate notarial wording on the document or attach a preprinted, "loose" certificate.

If the signer does not know what type of notarization is required, he or she should contact the document's issuing or receiving agency to determine this. This decision is *never* the Notary's to make unless the Notary is also an attorney.

11. Be attentive to details.

When filling out the certificate, the Notary needs to make sure the venue correctly identifies the place of notarization; if the venue is preprinted and incorrect, the Notary must line through the incorrect state and/or county, write in the proper site of the notarization and initial the change.

Also, the Notary must pay attention to spaces on the notarial certificate that indicate the number and gender of the document signers, as well as how they were identified — for example, leave the plural "(s)" untouched or cross it out, as appropriate.

12. Affix your signature and seal properly.

Notaries should sign *exactly* the same name appearing on their commissioning papers. The seal, if used, should be placed as close to the Notary's signature as possible without overprinting it. To prevent illegibility, a Notary seal should not be affixed over wording, particularly over a signature. Although an embossment may be placed over the letters "L.S.," an inked seal should be affixed next to but not over the letters to ensure legibility of the data in the seal. New York and several other states do not require Notaries to use seals; however, Notaries may be asked to write, type or stamp required wording on the certificate.

13. Protect loose certificates.

If the Notary has to attach a notarial certificate, it must be securely stapled to the left margin of the document. Notaries can protect against the removal of a loose certificate by embossing it together with the document and writing the particulars of the document to which the certificate is attached on the certificate. For example, the notation, "This certificate is attached to a 15-page partnership agreement between John Smith and Mary Doe, signed July 14, 1998," would deter fraudulent removal and reattachment of a loose certificate.

14. Don't give advice.

Every state prohibits nonattorneys from practicing law. Notaries should *never* prepare or complete documents for others, nor give advice on any matter relating to a document unless they are attorneys or professionals certified or licensed in a relevant area of expertise. The nonattorney Notary *never* chooses the type of certificate or notarization a document needs, since this decision can have important legal ramifications. The Notary could be held liable for any damages resulting from an incorrectly chosen certificate or notarization. ∎

Notary Laws Explained

In layperson's language, this chapter discusses and clarifies key parts of the current laws of New York that regulate Notaries Public, as compiled by the New York Department of State in the *Notary Public License Law* (NPLL), which is reprinted starting on page 73.

This edition of the *New York Notary Law Primer* also explains significant changes to New York law. The most notable of these changes prescribes new notarial certificates: an "all-purpose" acknowledgment and a form for a proof of execution by subscribing witness.

THE NOTARY COMMISSION

Application for New Commission

Qualifications. To become a first-time Notary in New York, the applicant must: (Executive Law, Section 130)

1) Be at least 18 years old;

2) Be a resident of New York State or maintain a place of business or office in the state; and

3) Complete and pass the New York State Notary Public examination.

Citizenship. Although New York Executive Law, Section 130, states that an applicant must be a U.S. citizen, this is not enforced. A 1984 Supreme Court decision, *Bernal v. Fainter*, declared that no state may deny a Notary commission merely on the basis of lack of U.S. citizenship.

Rejection of Application. The Department of State may reject an application for:

1) A conviction for a felony or certain other crimes, including using or carrying a firearm, buying or receiving stolen property, unlawful entry, drug-related offenses and prostitution; (Executive Law, Section 130)

2) Removal from office as a commissioner of deeds for the city of New York; (Executive Law, Section 140)

3) Violation of the Selective Draft Act of 1917, or of subsequent amending or supplementing laws, through such actions as evading the draft for military service. (Public Officers Law, Section 3)

May Not Be a Sheriff. Because sheriffs are barred from holding another public office, they may not be commissioned as a Notary Public. (Art. XIII, Section 13[a] of the Constitution of the State of New York)

Application Fee. A nonrefundable application fee of $30 shall be submitted with the application. An additional fee of $15 will be required at the time of examination. (Executive Law, Section 131)

Application for Reappointment

Reappointment. Notaries seeking reappointment must submit their applications to the local County Clerk, not the Department of State. No exam is required for reappointment.

The application may be picked up at the County Clerk's office or at a regional office of the Department of State (or call 1-518-474-4429 to have it mailed). The application must be completed in ink and its oath of office portion notarized.

Submit the application and the nonrefundable $30 fee to the County Clerk. No additional fees are required. (Executive Law, Section 131)

Proctored Exam

Required. All first-time Notary commission applicants — and applicants whose commissions have lapsed for more than six months — must complete and pass a proctored, written examination prescribed by the Department of State, Division of Licensing Services. Applicants seeking to renew their commissions and former New York Notaries whose commissions have expired no more than six months prior to application are exempt from the exam. (Executive Law, Section 130)

Thumbprints

Required. All New York Notary applicants will be thumbprinted at the time of the Notary examination.

Notary Bond

Not Required. New York Notaries are not required to obtain a surety bond.

Liable for All Damages. New York Notaries have unlimited financial liability for any and all damages caused by their mistakes or misconduct in performing notarial acts. If a person is financially injured by a Notary's negligence or failure to properly perform a notarial act, whether intentional or unintentional, the injured party may sue the Notary in civil court and the Notary, possibly, may be ordered to pay all resulting damages, including attorney's fees. (Executive Law, Section 135)

Oath of Office

Requirement. New York Notaries are required to take and file an oath of office before executing any acts as a Notary Public. (Executive Law, Section 131)

Filing the Oath. The oath must be taken and filed with the Department of State — along with the applicant's original exam slip (marked "Passed") and completed application — within two years of the exam date. The oath must be notarized on the application. (Executive Law, Section 131)

To take the oath, the applicant must take the application form to a commissioned Notary, who will administer the required wording:

> I do solemnly swear (or affirm) that I will support the Constitution of the United States and the Constitution of the State of New York, and that I will faithfully discharge the duties of the office of Notary Public for the State of New York according to the best of my ability.

The applicant must repeat these words or say, "I will." The Notary administering the oath to the Notary applicant may not charge a fee. (Public Officers Law, Section 69)

If the application is for a renewal of a commission, the applicant must submit all necessary documents, including the application with a notarized oath, to the local County Clerk instead of the Department of State. (Executive Law, Section 131)

Jurisdiction

Statewide. New York Notaries may perform official acts throughout the state of New York but not beyond the state borders. They are not limited just to the respective counties where they live or work. The Notary may not witness a signing outside of New York State and then return to the state to perform the notarization. All parts of a given notarization must be performed at the same time and place within the state of New York. (Executive Law, Section 130)

Qualification as a Connecticut Notary. Residents of New York State who maintain or are regularly employed in an office in Connecticut may qualify for a Connecticut Notary commission. For more information, contact: Office of the Secretary of State, Records and Legislative Services Division, Notary Public Unit, 30 Trinity St., Hartford, CT 06106; or call 1-860-566-5273.

Qualification as a New Jersey Notary. Residents of New York State who maintain or are regularly employed in an office in New Jersey may qualify for a New Jersey Notary commission. For more information, contact: New Jersey Department of State, Division of Commercial Recording, Notary Public Section, CN-452, Trenton, NJ 08625; or call 1-609-530-6421.

Term of Office

Two-Year Term. The term of office for a New York State Notary Public is two years. Each term begins with the date specified by the Department of State and ends at midnight on its commission expiration date. (Executive Law, Section 130)

Resignation

Procedure. To resign, a Notary should submit a written notice to the Department of State, giving an effective date. Such a resignation is appropriate if the Notary moves and does not retain a place of business or office in New York State. It is recommended that the notice be sent by certified mail.

The resignation notice may also be sent to the office of the County Clerk where the Notary has qualified or filed certificates of official character.

If the resigning Notary has a seal of office or a stamp used to affix information on certificates, these should be destroyed or defaced to prevent fraudulent use.

Public-Employee Notaries

Appointment by County Clerk. Each County Clerk is required to designate at least one member of his or her staff to act as a Notary Public. The Notary Public will be available in each County Clerk's office to notarize documents for the public during normal business hours. (Public Officers Law, Section 534)

No Commission Fees. Such public-employee designees will be exempt from Notary commission examination and application fees. (Public Officers Law, Section 534)

Notary Fees. No fees may be collected for notarial acts performed by a public-employee Notary.

Change of Address

Notification. The New York Department of State should be informed of any change in the Notary's residence, office or place of business. (Executive Law, Section 131)

Retaining the Commission. A New York Notary who moves his or her residence out of New York State, but still maintains a place of business or an office in New York State, may retain the Notary commission. However, if both residence and office or place of business move out of state or are eliminated, the Notary's commission will be terminated.

Likewise, the commission of a New York Notary who does not live in New York State and ceases to have an office or place of business in the state will be terminated. (Executive Law, Section 130)

Fee. When notified by a Notary of a change of address, the Department of State will impose an administrative fee of $10 on the Notary. This fee will not be imposed when such change is made on an application for reappointment. (Executive Law, Section 131)

Change of Name

Notification. The New York Department of State should be informed of any change of name by the Notary.

Change of Name by Marriage. When a Notary marries during an appointed two-year term of office, the Notary may continue to use the maiden or original name in the official signature and seal. If the Notary elects to use the new married name, however, this Notary must continue to use the maiden or original name in the signature and seal, but add the new married name in parentheses after the signature.

Upon renewing, the Notary may then apply for a new commission using either the maiden or original name, or the new married name. (NPLL, "Definitions and General Terms")

Religious Name. If a person has taken and is known by a name given by a religious order, that individual may be appointed as a New York State Notary Public and officiate as such using the given religious name. (NPLL, "Definitions and General Terms")

Fee. When notified by a Notary of a change of name, the Department of State will impose an administrative fee of $10 on the Notary. This fee will not be imposed when such changes are made on an application for reappointment. (Executive Law, Section 131)

OFFICIAL NOTARIAL ACTS

Authorized Acts

Notaries may perform the following official acts:

• Acknowledgments, certifying that a signer personally appeared before the Notary, was identified by the Notary, and acknowledged freely signing the document. See pages 24–28. (Executive Law, Section 135)

• Depositions, certifying that the spoken words of a witness were accurately taken down in writing, though this act is most often done by skilled court reporters. See pages 29–31. (Executive Law, Section 135)

• <u>Jurats</u>, as found in affidavits and other sworn documents, certifying that the signer personally appeared before the Notary, took an oath or affirmation from the Notary and, usually, signed in the Notary's presence. See pages 31–32. (Executive Law, Section 135)

• <u>Oaths and Affirmations</u>, which are solemn promises to God (oath) or solemn promises on one's own personal honor (affirmation). See pages 32–34. (Public Officers Law, Section 10, Executive Law, Section 135)

• <u>Proofs of Execution</u>, certifying that a subscribing witness personally appeared and swore to the Notary that another person, the principal, signed a document. See pages 34–37. (Real Property Law, Sections 304, 306)

• <u>Protests</u>, certifying that a written promise to pay, such as a bill of exchange, was not honored. See page 37. (Executive Law, Section 135)

• <u>Safe Deposit Box Openings</u> by a bank must be witnessed by Notaries. See pages 37–38. (Banking Law, Section 335)

Unauthorized Acts

<u>Certified Copies</u>. A certified copy is a duplicate of an original document that is certified as an exact reproduction. In New York, a Notary has no statutory authority to issue certified copies, nor to authenticate legal documents and other papers that will be filed with consular offices. (NPLL, "Definitions and General Terms")

Request for certified copies should be directed to the agency that holds or issued the original. For example, a certified copy of a birth certificate can be obtained from the Bureau of Vital Statistics (or the equivalent) in the state where the person was born.

An alternative to a Notary-certified copy is a copy certification by document custodian. Here the permanent keeper of a document — the custodian — certifies the duplicate in a written statement and the Notary executes a jurat for the custodian's signature. See "Copy Certification by Document Custodian," pages 28–29. (NPLL, "Definitions And General Terms")

Foreign-Language Documents. State law does not directly address the notarization of documents written in a language other than English, but it does set restrictions on the recording of such documents. See page 58. (Real Property Law, Section 333)

Marriages. New York State Notaries have no authority to perform marriages unless they are also ministers. (Domestic Relations Law, Section 11)

Notary's Own Signature. Although not directly addressed by New York law, a Notary must never notarize his or her own signature. The Department of State, however, does direct Notaries not to take acknowledgment of documents to which they are a party, nor to administer oaths to themselves. (NPLL, "Definitions and General Terms")

Telephone Notarizations. Notarizations — including acknowledgments and jurats — performed over the telephone are absolutely forbidden. A document signer *must* personally appear before the Notary, face to face in the same room, at the time of the notarization, not before, not after. (NPLL, "Definitions and General Terms," "Professional Conduct")
In addition, notarization based on a Notary's recognition of a signature, or on the unsworn word of a third party, without the signer's appearance before the Notary, is forbidden.

Wills. Notaries may not draft wills or offer legal advice about wills. However, if instructed to do so, the Notary may notarize the signatures of witnesses to self-proving wills. See pages 60–61. (NPLL, "Professional Conduct" and "Restrictions and Violations")

Acknowledgments
A Common Notarial Act. Acknowledgments are one of the most common forms of notarization. Typically, they are executed on deeds and other documents affecting real property that will be publicly recorded by a county official. (Executive Law, Section 135)

Purpose. In executing an acknowledgment, a Notary certifies three things: (Executive Law, Section 135)

1) The signer *personally appeared* before the Notary on the date and in the county indicated on the notarial certificate (notarization cannot be based on a telephone call or on a Notary's familiarity with a signature);

2) The signer was *positively identified* by the Notary through either personal knowledge or satisfactory evidence (see "Identifying Document Signers," page 38); and

3) The signer *acknowledged* to the Notary that the signature was freely made for the purposes stated in the document. (If a document is willingly signed in the presence of the Notary, this tacit act can serve just as well as an oral statement of acknowledgment.)

Certificate of Acknowledgment. Upon taking the acknowledgment of any document signer, the Notary must complete an appropriate certificate of acknowledgment. The certificate wording will either be printed at the end of the document, or appear on an attachment (a "loose" certificate) that is stapled to the document's signature page. (Real Property Law, Section 306)

New York statute prescribes a so-called "all-purpose" acknowledgment certificate (below) that may be used for signers who are acknowledging as an individual or in any representative capacity, including attorney in fact and partner, just to name a few.

Although prescribed by New York's Real Property Law, the all-purpose certificate may be used on documents not affecting real property.

A certificate of acknowledgment for an individual, a partner or a signer in any other representative capacity may be "substantially" in the following form, as prescribed by Section 309-a of the Real Property Law, until September 1, 1999, when it must be in the following form:

```
State of New York      )
                       ) ss.:
County of _____ )
```

On the _____ day of _____ in the year _____ before me, the undersigned, a Notary Public in and for said state, personally appeared _____, personally known to me or proved to me on the basis of satisfactory evidence to be the individual(s) whose name(s) is (are) subscribed to the within instrument and acknowledged to me that he/she/they executed the same in his/her/their capacity(ies), and that by his/her/their signature(s) on the instrument, the individual(s), or the person upon behalf of which the individual(s) acted, executed the instrument.

_____ (Signature of Notary)   (Seal of Notary, if any)

(Other required data printed, typewritten or stamped)

Alternate Certificates for Acknowledgment by Corporation.

Before September 1, 1999, the following acknowledgment certificates, or certificates that are substantially similar, must be used for acknowledgments involving corporations. The acknowledgment must be made by an officer or attorney in fact appointed by the corporation. (Real Property Law, Section 309)

On or after September 1, 1999, however, only the "all-purpose" acknowledgement form prescribed by Real Property Law Section 309-a may be used for corporate acknowledgers or any other representative acknowledgers on documents affecting real estate in New York State.

Although prescribed by New York's Real Property Law, these corporate acknowledgment certificates are routinely used on documents not affecting real property.

State of New York   )
) ss.:
County of _____)

On the _____ day of _____ in the year _____ before me personally came _____, to me known, who, being by me duly sworn, did depose and say that he/she/they reside(s) in _____ (if the place of residence is in a city, include the street and street number, if any, thereof); that he/she/they is (are) the (president or other officer or director or attorney in fact duly appointed) of the (name of corporation), the corporation described in and which executed the above instrument; that he/she/they know(s) the seal of said corporation; that the seal affixed to said instrument is such corporate seal; that it was so affixed by authority of the board of directors of said corporation, and that he/she/they signed his/her/their name(s) thereto by like authority.

_____ (Signature of Notary)   (Seal of Notary, if any)

(Other required data printed, typewritten or stamped)

State of New York   )
) ss.:
County of _____)

On the _____ day of _____ in the year
_____ before me personally came _____, to me
known, who, being by me duly sworn, did depose and say that
he/she/they reside(s) in _____ (if the place of residence is in
a city, include the street and street number, if any, thereof); that
he/she/they is (are) the (president or other officer or director or
attorney in fact duly appointed) of the (name of corporation), the
corporation described in and which executed the above instrument;
and that he/she/they signed his/her/their name(s) thereto by authority
of the board of directors of said corporation.

_____ (Signature of Notary)   (Seal of Notary, if any)

(Other required data printed, typewritten or stamped)

Identification of Acknowledger. In executing an
acknowledgment, the Notary must identify the signer through
personal knowledge, a credible identifying witness or
identification documents. See "Identifying Document Signers,"
page 38. (Real Property Law, Section 303)

Representative Capacity. If the so-called "all-purpose"
acknowledgment certificate prescribed by Section 309-a of New
York's Real Property Law is used, the Notary Public need not
ascertain that the signer holds the representative capacity claimed,
since the form does not state the exact capacity of the signer.
However, nothing prevents the careful Notary from asking a
representative signer for documentary proof that he or she actually
holds the capacity claimed. For an attorney in fact, this proof might
be the power of attorney naming the attorney in fact as an agent
for the principal; for a partner, it might be the written agreement
that formed the partnership; and for a corporate officer, it might be
the board of director's written order appointing the signer as a
corporate agent. (A business card by itself does not constitute
adequate documentary proof of a signer's representative status.)

Because New York's "all-purpose" acknowledgment certificate
does not state the signer's exact capacity, it is important that this
capacity be explicitly stated somewhere on the notarized
document or certificate. An attorney in fact, for example, might
clarify whom he or she is representing by signing the document
in the following or a similar manner: "Michael S. Jones, Attorney
in Fact for Diane A. Jones, Principal."

Witnessing of Signature Not Required. For an acknowledgment, the document does *not* have to be signed in the Notary's presence; however, the signer must appear before the Notary at the time of notarization to *acknowledge having signed the document.*

A document could have been signed an hour before, a week before, a year before, etc. — as long as the signer appears before the Notary with the signed document at the time of notarization to admit that the signature is his or her own. (However, for a jurat notarization, requiring an oath, the document usually must be signed in the presence of the Notary. See "Jurats," pages 31–32.)

Terminology. In discussing acknowledgments, it is important to use proper terms. A Notary *takes* or *executes* an acknowledgment, while a document signer *makes* or *gives* an acknowledgment.

Who May Take. In addition to a Notary, the following officials may take, anywhere in the state, acknowledgments and proofs relating to real estate: a supreme court justice, a title examiner and an official referee.

Other officials — such as a court judge, a commissioner of deeds, a mayor or city recorder, a surrogate, or a County Clerk — may take acknowledgments in their respective districts.

Certain other town or village officials may also take acknowledgments in the towns or villages where they perform their official duties. (Real Property Law, Section 298)

Married Women. A woman's marital status has no effect on her acknowledgment before a Notary. A Notary takes the acknowledgment made by a married woman in the same manner as if she were unmarried. (Real Property Law, Section 302)

Copy Certification by Document Custodian

Purpose. While not an official notarial act, copy certification by document custodian *may* serve as an alternative to a Notary-certified document copy when it is unlawful for the original document to be copied or certified by the Notary.

It should be noted that copy certification by document custodian may not always be an acceptable substitute for a Notary-certified copy, so the person requesting the act should check to be sure that it will serve the required purpose.

Procedure. The permanent keeper of the document — the

document custodian — *not* the Notary, certifies the copy. The custodian makes a photocopy of the original document; makes a written statement about the trueness, correctness and completeness of the copy; signs that statement before a Notary; and takes an oath or affirmation regarding the truth of the statement. The Notary, having witnessed the signing and given the oath or affirmation, executes a jurat.

Not for Vital Records. Copy certification by document custodian is not appropriate for vital records — such as birth, marriage and death certificates — since originals of these documents are retained by public agencies. Persons requesting certified copied of vital records should be directed to the agency that holds the original — typically, the Bureau of Vital Statistics or County Clerk in the area where the event occurred.

Certificate for Copy Certification by Document Custodian. In addition to the jurat certificate, the custodian's statement is required. Although not prescribed by law, this wording is recommended by the National Notary Association:

State of New York   )
) ss.:
County of _____)

I, _____ (name of custodian of original document), hereby swear (or affirm) that the attached reproduction of _____ (description of original document) is a true, correct and complete photocopy of a document in my possession.

_____ (signature of custodian) _____ (address)

Subscribed and sworn (or affirmed) before me this _____ day of _____ (month), _____ (year), by _____ (name of custodian).

_____ (Signature of Notary)   (Seal of Notary, if any)

(Other required data printed, typewritten or stamped)

Depositions and Affidavits

Purpose. A deposition is a signed transcript of the signer's oral statements taken down for use in a judicial proceeding. The deposition signer is called the *deponent.*

An affidavit is a signed statement made under oath or

affirmation by a person called an *affiant*, and it may be used for a variety of purposes both in and out of court.

For both a deposition and an affidavit, the Notary must administer an oath or affirmation and complete some form of jurat, which the Notary signs and seals.

Depositions. With a deposition, both sides in a lawsuit or court case have the opportunity to cross-examine the deponent. Questions and answers are transcribed into a written statement. Used only in judicial proceedings, a deposition is then signed and sworn to before an oath-administering official. (NPLL, "Definitions and General Terms")

New York Notaries have the power to take depositions — meaning, to transcribe the words spoken aloud by a deponent — but this duty is most often executed by trained and certified shorthand reporters, also known as court reporters. While most Notaries do not have the stenographic skills necessary to transcribe a deponent's words, any Notary is competent to administer an oath (or affirmation) or to execute a jurat on an existing deposition. (Executive Law, Section 135)

While the New York Civil Practice Law and Rules (Rule 3113) allows a Notary to take a deposition in a civil lawsuit, a deposition may not be taken on Sunday in such a civil proceeding. This rule, however, does not prohibit Notaries from otherwise administering oaths and taking affidavits and acknowledgments on Sunday. (NPLL, "Definitions and General Terms")

Affidavits. Affidavits are used in and out of court for a variety of purposes, from declaring losses to an insurance company to declaring U.S. citizenship before traveling to a foreign country. An affidavit is a document containing a statement voluntarily signed and sworn to or affirmed before a Notary or other official with oath-administering powers. If used in a judicial proceeding, only one side in the case need participate in the execution of the affidavit, in contrast to the deposition.

In an affidavit, the Notary's certificate typically sandwiches the affiant's signed statement, with the venue and affiant's name at the top of the document and the jurat wording at the end. The Notary is responsible for the venue, affiant's name and any notarial text at the beginning and end of the affidavit, and the affiant is responsible for the signed statement in the middle. (NPLL, "Definitions and General Terms")

Certificate for Depositions and Affidavits. Depositions and affidavits require jurat certificates. See "Jurats," pages 31–32.

Oath (Affirmation) for Depositions and Affidavits. If no other wording is prescribed in a given instance, a Notary may use the following language in administering an oath (or affirmation) for an affidavit or deposition:

> Do you solemnly swear that the contents of this affidavit (or deposition) subscribed by you is correct and true to the best of your knowledge and belief, so help you God?

> (Do you solemnly, sincerely and truly declare and affirm that the statements made by you are true and correct to the best of your knowledge and belief?)

For both oath and affirmation, the affiant must respond aloud and affirmatively, with "I do" or similar words. (NPLL, "Professional Conduct" and "Definitions and General Terms")

Jurats

Part of Verification. In notarizing affidavits, depositions and other forms of written verification requiring an oath by the signer, the Notary normally executes a jurat.

Purpose. While the purpose of an acknowledgment is to positively identify a document signer, the purpose of a verification with jurat is to compel truthfulness by appealing to the signer's conscience and fear of criminal penalties for perjury.

In executing a jurat, a Notary certifies that: (Executive Law, Section 135)

1) The signer *personally appeared* before the Notary at the time of notarization on the date and in the county indicated (notarization based on a telephone call or on familiarity with a signature is not acceptable);

2) The Notary *watched the signature* being made at the time of notarization, unless not stipulated by the jurat wording; and

3) The Notary *administered an oath* or affirmation to the signer.

Certificate for a Jurat. A typical jurat is the wording,

"Subscribed and sworn to (or affirmed) before me on this
_____ (date) by _____ (name of signer)..." or similar
language. "Subscribed" means "signed."

When jurat wording is not prescribed in a given instance, the
National Notary Association recommends the following:

State of New York   )
) ss.:
County of _____)

Subscribed and sworn to (or affirmed) before me this _____ day of
_____ (month), _____ (year), by _____ (name of signer).

_____ (Signature of Notary)   (Seal of Notary)

Other required data printed, typewritten or stamped)

Identification. Even though not required by law, the prudent
Notary will also take pains to positively identify each signer (as
is required by law for an acknowledgment).

Wording for Jurat Oath (Affirmation). If not otherwise prescribed
by law, a New York Notary may use the following or similar
words to administer an oath (or affirmation) in conjunction with
a jurat:

Do you solemnly swear that the statements in this document are true
to the best of your knowledge and belief, so help you God?

(Do you solemnly affirm that the statements in this document are true
to the best of your knowledge and belief?)

Oath or Affirmation Must Be Administered. A Notary Public
does not execute a jurat merely by asking whether or not the
signature on an affidavit is that of the signer. An oath or
affirmation must be administered and, usually, the affixation of
the signature observed by the Notary. (NPLL, "Definitions and
General Terms")

Oaths and Affirmations

Purpose. An oath is a solemn, spoken pledge to a Supreme
Being. An affirmation is a solemn, spoken pledge on one's own
personal honor, with no reference to a Supreme Being. Both are
usually a promise of truthfulness or fidelity and have the same
legal effect.

In taking an oath or affirmation in an official proceeding, a person may be subject to criminal penalties for perjury should he or she fail to be truthful.

An oath or affirmation can be a full-fledged notarial act in its own right, as when giving an oath of office to a public official ("swearing in" a public official), or it can be part of the process of notarizing a document (e.g., executing a jurat, or swearing in a credible identifying witness).

A person who objects to taking an oath — pledging to a Supreme Being — may instead be given an affirmation.

Power to Administer. New York Notaries may administer any oath required by state law, including oaths of office to public officials. (Public Officers Law, Section 10)

Wording for Oath (Affirmation). If law does not dictate otherwise, a New York Notary may use the following or similar words in administering an oath (or affirmation):

- Oath (Affirmation) for affiant signing an affidavit or deposition:

Do you solemnly swear that the statements in this document are true to the best of your knowledge and belief, so help you God?

(Do you solemnly affirm that the statements in this document are true to the best of your knowledge and belief?)

- Oath (Affirmation) for credible identifying witness(es):

Do you solemnly swear that you know this signer truly is the person he/she claims to be, so help you God?

(Do you solemnly affirm that you know this signer truly is the person he/she claims to be?)

- Oath (Affirmation) for subscribing witness(es):

Do you solemnly swear that you saw (name of the document signer) sign his/her name to this document and/or that he/she acknowledged to you having executed it for the purposes therein stated, so help you God?

(Do you solemnly affirm that you saw [name of document signer] sign his/her name to this document and/or that he/she acknowledged to you having executed it for the purposes therein stated?)

The person taking the oath or affirmation must respond by repeating these words or answering affirmatively with, "I do," "Yes," or similar words. A nod or grunt is not a clear and sufficient response. If a person is mute and unable to speak, the Notary may rely on written notes to communicate.

Ceremony and Gestures. To impress upon the oath-taker or affirmant the importance of truthfulness, the Notary is encouraged to lend a sense of ceremony and formality to the oath or affirmation. During administration of the oath or affirmation, the Notary and the document signer traditionally raise their right hands, though this is not a legal requirement. Notaries generally have discretion to use words and gestures they feel will most compellingly appeal to the conscience of the oath-taker or affiant. (NPLL, "Professional Conduct" and "Definitions and General Terms")

Oaths Are Personal. Only an individual may take an oath (or affirmation). An individual may not take an oath or affirmation in a representative capacity for another person.

In addition, an entity — such as a corporation or a partnership — may not take an oath or affirmation; however, a person representing a corporation, partnership or other legal entity may take an oath or affirmation as an individual, swearing that he or she has the authority to sign for the entity.

Not by Telephone. An oath (or affirmation) may not be given over the telephone. The oath-taker must physically appear in front of the Notary. In addition, a Notary may not administer an oath (or affirmation) to himself or herself. (NPLL, "Definitions and General Terms")

Oath or Affirmation Not Administered. Failure to administer any oath or affirmation as required by law may subject the Notary to being charged with a misdemeanor. (NPLL, "Restrictions and Violations")

Proof of Execution by Subscribing Witness

Purpose. In executing a proof of execution by subscribing witness, a Notary certifies that the signature of a person who does not appear before the Notary — the principal signer — is genuine and freely made based on the sworn testimony of another person who does appear — a subscribing (signing) witness.

Proofs of execution are used when the principal signer is out of town or otherwise unavailable to appear before a Notary. Because of their high potential for fraudulent abuse, proofs of execution are not universally accepted, though they are legal for the New York Notary to perform. Proofs should only be used as a last resort and never merely because the principal signer prefers not to take the time to personally appear before a Notary.

In Lieu of Acknowledgment. On recordable documents, a proof of execution by a subscribing witness is usually regarded as an acceptable substitute for an acknowledgment.

New York State law authorizes Notaries to execute proofs of execution in place of acknowledgments. (Real Property Law, Section 304)

Subscribing Witness. A subscribing witness is a person who watches a principal sign a document (or who personally takes the principal's acknowledgment) and then subscribes (signs) his or her own name on the document at the principal's request and in the principal's presence. This witness brings that document to a Notary on the principal's behalf and takes an oath or affirmation from the Notary to the effect that the principal is known to him or her, and did indeed willingly sign (or acknowledge signing) the document and request the witness to also sign the document and bring it to a Notary.

The ideal subscribing witness personally knows the principal signer and has no personal beneficial or financial interest in the document or transaction. It would be foolish of the Notary, for example, to rely on the word of a subscribing witness presenting for notarization a power of attorney that names this very witness as attorney in fact.

Oath (Affirmation) for Subscribing Witness. An acceptable oath for the subscribing witness might be:

> Do you solemnly swear that you saw (name of the document signer) sign his/her name to this document and/or that he/she acknowledged to you having executed it for the purposes therein stated, so help you God?
>
> (Do you solemnly affirm that you saw [name of document signer] sign

his/her name to this document and/or that he/she acknowledged to you having executed it for the purposes therein stated?)

The subscribing witness should then sign the Notary's journal (if one is kept) and the Notary completes a proof of execution by subscribing witness certificate, often called a witness jurat.

Identifying Subscribing Witness. Since the Notary is relying entirely on the word of the subscribing witness to vouch for an absent signer's identity, willingness and general competency, it is best for subscribing witnesses to be personally known to the Notary. New York law, however, allows the Notary to identify a subscribing witness through satisfactory evidence (documentary identification or a credible identifying witness). (Real Property Law, Section 304)

Whether or not the Notary personally knows the subscribing witness, the subscribing witness must personally know the principal. (Real Property Law, Section 304)

Certificate for Proof of Execution. In executing a proof of execution on a document affecting real property in New York State, a New York Notary *may* use the following certificate. Any other form used must state the subscribing witness's residence, including exact street address. (Real Property Law, Section 306)

However, for proofs taken on or after September 1, 1999, the following certificate, or one that is "substantially" similar, *must* be used. (Real Property Law, Section 309-a)

Although prescribed by New York's Real Property Law, these certificates may be used on documents not affecting real property.

State of New York)
) ss.:
County of _____)

On the _____ day of _____ in the year _____ before me, the undersigned, a Notary Public in and for said State, personally appeared _____, the subscribing witness to the foregoing instrument, with whom I am personally acquainted, who, being by me duly sworn, did depose and say that he/she/they reside(s) in _____ (if the place of residence is in a city, include the street and street number, if any, thereof); that he/she/they know(s) _____ to be the individual described in and who executed the foregoing instrument; that said subscribing witness was present and saw said _____ execute the same; and that said witness at the same time subscribed his/her/their name(s) as a witness thereto.

_____ (Signature of Notary)   (Seal of Notary, if any)

(Other required data, printed, typewritten or stamped)

Protests

Purpose. In rare instances, Notaries may be asked to protest a negotiable instrument for nonpayment. A protest is a written statement by a Notary or other authorized officer verifying that payment was not received on an instrument such as a bank draft. Failure to pay is called *dishonor.*

Before issuing a certificate of protest, the Notary must present the bank draft or other instrument to the person, firm or institution obligated to pay, a procedure called *presentment.*

Antiquated Act. In the 19th century, protests were common notarial acts in the United States, but they rarely are performed today due to the advent of modern electronic communications and resulting changes in our banking and financial systems. Modern Notaries most often encounter protests in the context of international commerce.

Special Knowledge Required. Notarial acts of protest are complicated and varied, requiring a special knowledge of financial and legal terminology. Only Notaries who have the requisite knowledge, or who are acting under the supervision of an experienced bank officer or an attorney familiar with the Uniform Commercial Code, should attempt a protest.

Witnessing Safe Deposit Box Opening

May Witness Opening. If the rental fee on a safe deposit box has not been paid and the bank has attempted to contact the lessee without success, the bank may open and inventory the box in the presence of a Notary Public.

The Notary then issues a certificate stating the lessee's name, the date of the opening and a list of the contents in the box. Within 10 days of the opening, a copy of the certificate must be mailed by the owner of the safe deposit box to the lessee's last known address. (Banking Law, Section 335)

Certificate for Inventorying a Safe Deposit Box. New York law does not provide specific wording for the certificate. The following wording is suggested:

State of New York)
) ss.:
County of _____)

On the _____ (day) of _____ (month), _____ (year), safe
deposit box number _____, rented in the name of _____,
was opened by _____ (name of financial institution) in my
presence and in the presence of _____ (name of financial
institution officer). The contents of the box consisted of the following:

(list of contents)

_____ (Signature of financial institution officer)
_____ (Print or type name)
_____ (Signature of Notary)   (Seal of Notary, if any)
_____ (Name of Notary, printed, typed or stamped)

PRACTICES AND PROCEDURES

Identifying Document Signers

Acknowledgments. In taking the acknowledgment of a
signature on any document, New York law requires the Notary
to identify the acknowledger. The following three methods of
identification are acceptable: (Real Property Law, Section 303)

1) The Notary's *personal knowledge* of the signer's identity
(see "Personal Knowledge of Identity," pages 38–39); or

2) The oath or affirmation of a personally known *credible
identifying witness* (see "Credible Identifying Witness(es),"
pages 39–40); or

3) Reliable *identification documents* or ID cards (see
"Identification Documents (ID Cards)," pages 40–42).

Identification for Other Notarial Acts. While the law specifies
identification standards only for acknowledgers, the prudent and
conscientious Notary will apply these same standards in
identifying any signer, whether for an acknowledgment, a jurat or
any other notarial act.

Personal Knowledge of Identity

Definition. The safest and most reliable method of

identifying a document signer is for the Notary to depend on his or her own personal knowledge of the signer's identity. Personal knowledge means familiarity with an individual resulting from interactions with that person over a period of time sufficient to eliminate every reasonable doubt that the person has the identity claimed. The familiarity should come from association with the individual in relation to other people and should be based upon a chain of circumstances surrounding the individual.

New York law does not specify how long a Notary must be acquainted with an individual before personal knowledge of identity may be claimed. So, the Notary's common sense must prevail. In general, the longer the Notary is acquainted with a person, and the more random interactions the Notary has had with that person, the more likely the individual is indeed personally known.

For instance, the Notary might safely regard a friend since childhood as personally known, but would be foolish to consider a person met for the first time the previous day as such. Whenever the Notary has a reasonable doubt about a signer's identity, that individual should be considered not personally known, and the identification should be made through either a credible identifying witness or reliable identification documents. (Real Property Law, Section 303)

Credible Identifying Witness(es)

Purpose. When a document signer is not personally known to the Notary and is not able to present reliable ID cards, that signer may be identified on the oath (or affirmation) of a credible identifying witness.

Qualifications. Every credible identifying witness must personally know the document signer. The credible identifying witness must also be personally known by the Notary. This establishes a "chain of personal knowledge" from the Notary to the credible identifying witness to the signer. In a sense, a credible identifying witness is a walking, talking ID card.

Credible witnesses must never themselves be identified to the Notary through ID cards. Any credible identifying witness should have a reputation for honesty; the witness should be a competent, independent individual who won't be tricked, cajoled, bullied or otherwise influenced into identifying someone he or she does not really know. In addition, the witness should have no personal interest in the transaction requiring a notarial act.

Oath (Affirmation) for Credible Identifying Witness. To ensure truthfulness, the Notary must administer an oath or affirmation to each credible identifying witness.

If not otherwise prescribed by New York law, an acceptable credible-witness oath or affirmation might be:

> Do you solemnly swear you know that this signer is the person he/she claims to be, so help you God?

> (Do you solemnly affirm you know that this signer is the person he/she claims to be?)

Signature in Notary's Journal. If the Notary maintains a journal — although a journal is not required by law — each credible identifying witness should sign the Notary's journal, along with the document signer. The Notary should also print each witness's name and address.

Satisfactory Evidence. A credible identifying witness is generally regarded as a form of "satisfactory evidence" of identity that is equivalent to the Notary's personal knowledge of a signer's identity. Another form of satisfactory evidence of identity, of course, is a reliable government-issued ID card that bears the signer's photograph, signature and physical description. (Real Property Law, Section 303)

Not a Subscribing Witness. Do not confuse *credible identifying* witness(es) with *subscribing* witness(es). A credible identifying witness vouches for the identity of a signer who appears before the Notary. A subscribing witness vouches for the genuineness of the signature of a person who does not appear before the Notary. See "Proof of Execution by Subscribing Witness," pages 34–37.

Identification Documents (ID Cards)

Acceptable Identification Documents. Notaries customarily are allowed to use reliable identification documents (ID cards) to identify document signers whom they do not personally know. Such cards are considered to be "satisfactory evidence" of identity in lieu of personal knowledge, just as is the sworn word of a personally known credible identifying witness.

The best ID cards have three components: a photograph, a signature and a physical description (e.g., "brown hair, green eyes," etc.) of the bearer. Generally reliable forms of identification include: (Real Property Law, Section 303)

- New York driver's license or official nondriver's ID.

- U.S. and foreign passports.

- U.S. military ID.

- Resident alien ID, or "green card," issued by the Immigration and Naturalization Service (INS).

Multiple Identification. While one good identification document or card may be sufficient to identify a signer, the Notary is encouraged to ask for more.

Unacceptable Identification Documents. Identification documents that are not acceptable for identifying acknowledgers include Social Security cards, credit cards, temporary driver's licenses, driver's licenses without photographs and birth certificates.

Fraudulent Identification. Identification documents are the least secure of the three methods of identifying a document signer because phony ID cards are common. The Notary should scrutinize each card for evidence of tampering or counterfeiting, or for evidence that it is a genuine card that has been issued to an impostor.

Some clues that an ID card may have been fraudulently tampered with include: mismatched type styles, a photograph raised from the surface, a signature that does not match the signature on the document, unauthorized lamination of the card, and smudges, erasures, smears and discolorations.

Possible tip-offs to a counterfeit ID card include: misspelled words, a brand new-looking card with an old date of issuance, two cards with exactly the same photograph, and inappropriate patterns and features.

Some possible indications that a card may have been issued to

NEW YORK NOTARY LAW PRIMER

an impostor include: the card's birth date or address is unfamiliar
to the bearer, all the ID cards seem brand new, and the bearer is
unwilling to leave a thumbprint in the journal. (Such a print is not
required by law but is requested by some Notaries as protection
against forgers and lawsuits. Refusal to leave a thumbprint is not
in itself grounds to deny a notarization.)

Journal of Notarial Acts

Recommended. The National Notary Association and many
Notary-regulating officials across the nation strongly recommend
that every Notary keep a detailed, accurate and sequential
journal of notarial acts, though not required by law in New York.

Prudent Notaries keep detailed and accurate journals of their
notarial acts for many reasons:

• Keeping records is a *businesslike practice* that every
conscientious businessperson and public official should
engage in. Not keeping records of important transactions,
whether private or public, is risky.

• A Notary's recordbook *protects the public's rights* to
valuable property and to due process by providing
documentary evidence in the event a document is lost or
altered, or if a transaction is later challenged.

• In the event of a civil lawsuit alleging that the Notary's
negligence or misconduct caused the plaintiff serious financial
harm, a detailed journal of notarial acts can *protect the Notary*
by showing that reasonable care was used to identify a signer.
It would be difficult to contend that the Notary did not bother
to identify a signer if the Notary's journal contains a detailed
description of the ID cards that the signer presented.

• Since civil lawsuits arising from a contested notarial act
typically take place three to six years after the act occurs, the
Notary normally cannot accurately testify in court about the
particulars of a notarization without a journal to *aid the
Notary's memory.*

• Journals of notarial acts *prevent or abort baseless lawsuits* by
showing that a Notary did use reasonable care, or that a
transaction did occur as recorded. Journal fingerprints and

signatures are especially effective in defeating such groundless suits.

• Requiring each document signer to leave a signature, or even a fingerprint, in the Notary's journal both *deters attempted forgeries* and provides strong evidence for a conviction should a forgery occur.

Journal Entries. The Notary's recordbook should contain the following information for each notarial act performed:

1) The date, time of day and type of notarization (e.g., jurat, acknowledgment, etc.);

2) The type (or title) of document notarized (e.g., deed of trust, INS affidavit of support, etc.), including the number of pages and the date of the document;

3) The signature, address and printed name of each document signer and witness;

4) A statement as to how the signer's identity was confirmed (If by personal knowledge, the journal entry should read "Personal Knowledge." If by satisfactory evidence, the journal entry must contain either: a description of the ID card accepted, including the type of ID, the government agency issuing the ID, the serial or identifying number and the date of issuance or expiration; or the signature of any credible identifying witness and how that credible identifying witness was identified — see "Credible Identifying Witness(es)," pages 39–40); and

5) Any other pertinent information, including the fee charged for the notarial service or any peculiarities relating to the signer or the document.

Journal Thumbprint. Increasingly, Notaries are asking document signers to leave a thumbprint in the journal. The journal thumbprint is a strong deterrent to forgery, because it represents absolute proof of the forger's identity and appearance. Nothing prevents a Notary from asking for a thumbprint for every notarial act, if the signer is willing. However, the Notary may not make leaving a thumbprint a precondition for notarizing.

Complete Entry Before Certificate. The Notary should complete the journal entry before filling out the notarial certificate on a document to prevent the signer from leaving with the notarized document before vital information is entered in the journal.

Never Surrender Journal. Notaries should never surrender control of their journals to anyone, unless expressly subpoenaed by a court order. Even when an employer has paid for the Notary's official journal and seal, they go with the Notary upon termination of employment; no person but the Notary may properly possess and write in these records.

Notarial Certificate

Requirement. In notarizing any document, a Notary must complete a notarial certificate. The certificate is wording that indicates exactly what the Notary has certified. The notarial certificate wording may appear on the document itself or on an attachment to it. The certificate should contain:

1) A *venue* indicating where the notarization is being performed. "State of New York, County of _____," is the typical venue wording, with the county name inserted in the blank. The letters "SS." or "SCT." sometimes appear after the venue; they abbreviate the traditional Latin word *scilicet*, meaning "in particular" or "namely."

2) A *statement of particulars* that indicates what the notarization has attested. An acknowledgment certificate might include such wording as: "On _____ (date) before me, _____ (name of Notary), personally appeared, _____ (name of signer), personally known to me (or proved to me on the basis of satisfactory evidence) to be the person(s)..." A jurat certificate might include such wording as: "Subscribed and sworn to (or affirmed) before me this _____ (date) by _____ (name of signer)."

3) A *testimonium clause*, which may be optional if the date is included in the statement of particulars: "Witness my hand and official seal, this the _____ day of _____ (month),

_____ (year)." In this short sentence, the Notary formally attests to the truthfulness of the preceding facts in the certificate. "Hand" means signature.

4) The *official signature of the Notary*, exactly as the name appears on the Notary's commissioning paper.

5) The *seal of the Notary*, although not required by New York law. On many certificates the letters "L.S." appear, indicating where the seal is to be located. These letters abbreviate the Latin term *locus sigilli*, meaning "place of the seal." An inking seal should be placed near but not over the letters, so that wording imprinted by the seal will not be obscured. An embossing seal, used in conjunction with an inking seal, may be placed directly over the letters — slightly displacing portions of the characters and leaving a clue that document examiners can use to distinguish an original from a forged photocopy.

Depending on state law, additional information — similar to the information in a Notary's seal — is sometimes required. On each notarial certificate, a New York Notary is required to print, typewrite or stamp the following information in black ink: the Notary's name; the words "Notary Public State of New York"; the Notary's commission expiration date; and the name of the county in which the Notary was originally qualified.

Loose Certificates. When certificate wording is not preprinted on the document for the Notary to fill out, a "loose" certificate may be attached. Normally, this form is stapled to the document's left margin preceding or following the signature page. Only one side of the certificate should be stapled, so it can be lifted to show the document underneath.

To prevent a loose certificate from being removed and fraudulently placed on another document, there are precautions a Notary can take. The Notary can emboss the certificate and document together, writing, "Attached document bears embossment," on the certificate. Or the Notary can write a brief description of the document on the certificate: e.g., "This certificate is attached to a _____ (title or type of document), dated _____, or _____ (number) pages, also signed by _____ (name[s] of other signer[s])."

While fraud-deterrent steps such as these can make it much more difficult for a loose certificate to be removed and misused, there is no absolute protection against its removal and misuse. Notaries must absolutely ensure that while a certificate remains in their control, it is attached only to its intended document. A Notary must never give or mail a signed and sealed notarial certificate to another person and trust that person to attach it to a particular document; this would be an all but indefensible action in a civil court of law.

Do Not Pre-Sign/Seal Certificates. A Notary should never sign and/or seal certificates ahead of time or permit other persons to attach loose notarial certificates to documents. Nor should the Notary send an unattached, signed and sealed, loose certificate through the mail, even if requested to do so by a signer who previously appeared before the Notary. These actions may facilitate fraud or forgery, and they could subject the Notary to lawsuits to recover damages resulting from the Notary's neglect or misconduct.

Selecting Certificates. It is not the role of the Notary to decide what type of certificate — thus, what type of notarization — a document needs. As ministerial officials, Notaries generally follow instructions and fill out forms that have been provided for them; they do not issue instructions and decide which forms are appropriate in a given case.

If a document is presented to a Notary without certificate wording and if the signer doesn't know what type of notarization is appropriate, the signer should be asked to find out what kind of notarization and certificate are needed. Usually, the agency that issued the document or the one that will be accepting the document can provide this information. Selecting certificates is an unauthorized practice of law.

False Certificates. A Notary who knowingly completes a false notarial certificate may be guilty of a Class D Felony, punishable by a prison term of up to seven years, or a Class E Felony, for which a prison term of up to four years may be imposed.

A Notary would be completing a false certificate, for example, if he or she signed and sealed an acknowledgment certificate indicating a signer personally appeared when the signer actually did not. (Executive Law, Section 135-a)

Notaries are often pressured by employers, clients, friends or relatives to be untruthful in their official certificates. An employer may ask the Notary to notarize a spouse's signature without the spouse's presence; a client may ask the Notary to take an acknowledgment over the phone; a friend or relative may ask the Notary to consider a stranger as personally known. In complying with these requests, the Notary would have to fill out a false certificate, which is a criminal act.

Notary Seal

Recommended. The National Notary Association recommends that Notaries affix an impression of an official seal on the certificate portion of every document notarized, although New York law does not require Notaries to do so.

Affixing a seal impression is a convenient way for the Notary to include required information on the certificate (see "Required Information," pages 47–48). The seal also imparts an appropriate sense of ceremony to the notarial act.

Another practical reason for using a notarial seal is to prevent any rejection or delay of acceptance of notarized documents sent to other states and nations where use of seals is a normal practice. (NPLL, "Definitions and Terms")

Embossing and Inking Seals. The seal may be either an inking stamp or an embosser. The inking seal leaves a photographically reproducible impression; the embosser, a raised impression. (Many New York Notaries already use rubber stamps to affix their name, commission expiration date and certain other required information. See "Required Information, pages 47–48.)

In many states, county recording officials prefer inking seals because they considerably simplify the process of microfilming property deeds and other recordable documents. Recorders have to smudge seal embossments with carbon or other photocopiable substances before they can be microfilmed.

Format. The size and shape of the seal are left to the discretion of the Notary. By custom, most embossing seals are circular, and most inking seals are rectangular.

Required Information. The Department of State advises that the Notary seal should identify the Notary, his or her authority and jurisdiction. The Department requires the only wording to be the name of the Notary and the words "Notary Public for the State of New York." (NPLL, "Definitions and Terms")

However, the seal may also conveniently include the following information which must be printed, stamped or typed in black ink beneath the Notary's signature on every notarial certificate:

- The name of the Notary;

- The words "Notary Public State of New York" or, if applicable and preferred, "Attorney and Counsellor at Law State of New York";

- The name of the county where the Notary originally qualified;

- The Notary's commission expiration date; and

- Any additional required information, including but not limited to, the name of the county in which the Notary's certificate of official character is filed, using the words "Certificate filed _____ County". In addition, a Notary who has qualified or filed a certificate of official character in a county within the city of New York must affix any official number given to him or her by that county; and if a particular notarized document is to be recorded in any register's office in the city of New York, the Notary must also affix any official number that may have been given to the Notary by the register.

While the omission of the above information may not cause the invalidation of a particular notarized document, it may subject the Notary to disciplinary action by the New York Secretary of State. (Executive Law, Section 137)

Placement of Seal Impression. The Notary's seal impression should be placed near the Notary's signature on the notarial certificate. Whenever possible — and especially with documents that will be submitted to a recording official — the Notary should avoid affixing the seal over any text on the document or certificate. Some recorders will reject documents if writing or document text intrudes within the borders of the Notary's seal. If there is no room for required stamp information, the Notary may have no choice but to complete and attach a loose certificate that duplicates the notarial wording on the document. With documents that will *not* be publicly recorded, however, the recipient may allow the Notary to affix the stamp or seal over boilerplate text — the standard preprinted clauses or sections — as long as the wording within the stamp or seal is not obscured.

L.S. The letters "L.S." — from the Latin *locus sigilli*, meaning "location of the seal" — appear on many notarial certificates to indicate where the Notary seal should be placed. Only an embosser seal should be placed *over* these letters. An inking seal should be placed *near,* but not over, the letters.

Fees for Notarial Services

Maximum Fees. The following maximum fees for performing notarial acts are allowed by New York law:

- Acknowledgments — $2. For taking an acknowledgment, the fee is not to exceed $2 for each signature — that is, the acknowledger's signature, not the Notary's — plus $2 for each witness sworn in. For example, for notarizing a single document with signatures of three persons appearing before the Notary, a maximum of $6 could be charged. (Executive Law, Section 136)

- Oaths and Affirmations — $2. For administering an oath or affirmation, with or without a jurat certificate, the fee is not to exceed $2 per person, except where another fee is prescribed by statute. However, a Notary may not charge a fee for administering an oath of office to a member of the Legislature, to any military officer, to an inspector of elections, a clerk of the poll, or to any other public officer or public employee. (Executive Law, Section 136; Public Officers Law, Section 69)

- Protests — 75¢. For executing a protest for nonpayment or nonacceptance, the maximum fee is 75¢. For each notice of protest, not exceeding five notices on any bill or note, the fee is 10¢. (Executive Law, Section 135)

- Proofs of Execution by Subscribing Witness — $2. For

taking a proof of execution by a subscribing witness, the Notary may charge a maximum fee of $2 for each principal, plus $2 for swearing in the subscribing witness.

Option Not to Charge. Notaries are not required to charge for their notarial services. And they may charge any fee less than the maximum.

Overcharging. Charging more than the legally prescribed fees may subject the Notary to removal from office, criminal prosecution and civil action in which the person overcharged may seek triple the damages from the Notary. (Public Officers Law, Section 67)

Seal Affixed Free of Charge. A Notary may not charge any additional fee for affixing a seal on a certificate of protest or other notarial form. (Executive Law, Section 135)

No Fees Allowed for Certain Notaries. No fee may be charged by a Notary on the staff of a County Clerk who has been designated by law to notarize for the public during normal business hours. (Public Officers Law, Section 534)

Dividing Fees with Attorney. A New York Notary may not divide or agree to divide his or her fees with an attorney. In addition, the Notary may not accept any part of an attorney's fee for any legal business. (NPLL, "Professional Conduct")

Blank or Incomplete Documents

Do Not Notarize. While New York law does not specifically address notarizing a blank or incomplete document, this is a dangerous, unbusinesslike practice and a breach of common sense, similar to signing a blank check.

A fraudulent document could readily be created above a Notary's signed and sealed certificate on an otherwise blank paper. And, with documents containing blanks to be filled in after the notarization by a person other than the signer, there is a danger that the information inserted will be contrary to the wishes of the signer.

Any blanks in a document should be filled in by the signer. If the blanks are inapplicable and intended to be left unfilled, the signer should be asked to line through each space (using ink) or write "Not Applicable" or "NA."

False Documents

Notary Not Responsible. It is not the duty of the Notary to verify the truthfulness or accuracy of the facts in the text of a document. In fact, Notaries are not even required to read the documents they notarize. The Notary is entitled, though, to quickly scan the instrument to extract important particulars (its title, date and number of pages, for example) to record in an official recordbook.

However, if a Notary happens to discover that a document is false or fraudulent, the Notary as a responsible public official has a duty to refuse the notarization, and to report the attempted fraud to appropriate authorities. Indeed, according to the New York Department of State, for administering an oath on an affidavit statement that the Notary knows to be false, the Notary may be removed from office. (NPLL, "Definitions and General Terms")

Disqualifying Interest

Impartiality. Notaries are appointed by the state to be impartial, disinterested witnesses whose screening duties help ensure the integrity of important legal and commercial transactions. Lack of impartiality by a Notary throws doubt on the integrity and lawfulness of any transaction. A Notary must never notarize his or her own signature or notarize a transaction to which the Notary is a party or has a financial or beneficial interest.

Financial or Beneficial Interest. A financial or beneficial interest exists when the Notary is individually named as a principal in a financial transaction or when the Notary receives an advantage, right, privilege, property, or fee valued in excess of the lawfully prescribed notarial fee.

According to the New York Department of State, a Notary must not notarize if the Notary is a party to the document or if the Notary has a financial or beneficial interest in the document. This, for example, would disqualify a Notary who is a grantee or mortgagee in a conveyance or mortgage from taking the acknowledgment of the grantor or mortgagor.

New York courts have voided documents notarized by persons financially and beneficially interested in a related transaction.

Any challenged case of disqualifying financial or beneficial interest would be decided in court on its own merits. Thus, it is always safest for a Notary to have no financial or beneficial interest whatsoever in a transaction regardless of what the law allows. (NPLL, "Appointment and Qualifications")

Corporations. Corporate stockholders, directors, officers and employees may notarize for other stockholders, directors, officers and employees as long as the notarizing officer is not a party to the transaction. (Executive Law, Section 138)

Attorneys. Attorneys allowed to practice in New York State may, at their discretion, notarize for clients. (Executive Law, Section 135)

Relatives. State officials strongly discourage Notaries from notarizing for persons related by blood or marriage because of the likelihood of a financial or beneficial interest, whether large or small.

Often a Notary will have a clear-cut disqualifying financial or beneficial interest in notarizing for a close relative, especially with a spouse. If the Notary's spouse, for example, purchases a home in which the couple will live, then the Notary should not notarize the deed for the purchase.

It is often difficult for a Notary to retain impartiality with a close relative. Anyone, for example, is entitled to counsel a relative to sign or not to sign an important document, but such counseling is entirely inappropriate for the impartial Notary.

Refusal of Services

Legal Requests for Services. Notaries must honor all lawful and reasonable requests to notarize, whether or not the person requesting the act is a client or customer of the Notary or the Notary's employer. In addition, a person's race, religion, nationality or politics are not due cause for refusing to perform a notarial act. (Penal Law, Sections 70.15, 195.00)

Noncustomer Discrimination Prohibited. A Notary employed by a private employer should not discriminate between customers and noncustomers. Fees and services provided should be the same for all customers, whether or not the customer is a client of the employer.

Penalty. Should a Notary refuse to perform a notarial act

when lawfully requested, the Notary may be subject to charges of official misconduct. Such official misconduct is a Class A Misdemeanor for which a prison term of up to one year may be imposed. (Penal Law, Sections 70.15, 195.00)

Exception. A Notary may refuse to notarize a document if he or she knows that the document is blatantly fraudulent.

Reasonable Care

Responsibility. As public servants, Notaries must act responsibly and exercise reasonable care in the performance of their official duties. If a Notary fails to do so, he or she may be subject to a civil lawsuit to recover financial damages caused by the Notary's error or omission.

In general, reasonable care is that degree of concern and attentiveness that a person of normal intelligence and responsibility would exhibit. If a Notary can show to a judge or jury that he or she did everything expected of a reasonable person, the judge or jury is obligated by law to find the Notary blameless and not liable for damages.

Complying with all pertinent laws is the first rule of reasonable care for a Notary. And, if there are no statutory guidelines in a given instance, the Notary should go to extremes to use common sense and prudence. See "Steps to Proper Notarization," pages 13–16.

Records. Although not required by law, a Notary's best proof of having exercised reasonable care is a detailed, accurate journal of notarial acts. Such entries as the serial numbers of identification documents and the signatures of credible identifying witnesses can show that the Notary took steps to positively identify every signer. Possession by the Notary of a well-maintained recordbook can prevent lawsuits that falsely claim the Notary was negligent.

Unauthorized Practice of Law

Do Not Assist in Legal Matters. A Notary may not give legal advice or accept fees for legal advice. As a ministerial official, the nonattorney Notary is generally not permitted to assist other persons in drafting, preparing, selecting, completing or understanding a document or transaction.

The Notary should not fill in the blank spaces in the text of a document for other persons, tell others what documents they need or how to draft them, nor advise others about the legal sufficiency of a document — and especially not for a fee.

A Notary, of course, may fill in the blanks on the portion of any document containing the notarial certificate. And a Notary, as a private individual, may prepare legal documents that he or she is personally a party to; but the Notary may not then notarize his or her own signature on these same documents.

In New York State, the unauthorized practice of law is a misdemeanor. In addition, the state Supreme Court has the power to punish for criminal contempt any person who illegally practices law. As a result, the unauthorized practice of law by a Notary may cause the Notary to be removed from office by the Secretary of State, be imprisoned, or both. (Judiciary Law, Sections 484, 485, 750)

Do Not Determine Notarial Act. A Notary who is not an attorney should not determine the type of notarial act to perform or decide which certificate to attach. This is beyond the scope of the Notary's expertise and might be considered the unauthorized practice of law. The Notary should only follow instructions provided by the document, its signer, its issuing or receiving agency, or by an attorney.

If a document lacks notarial certificate wording, the Notary must ask the document signer what type of notarization — acknowledgment or jurat — is required. The Notary may then type the appropriate notarial wording on the document or attach a preprinted, loose certificate. If the signer does not know what type of notarization is required, the issuing or receiving agency should be contacted. This decision is *never* to be made by the Notary, unless the Notary is also an attorney.

Exceptions. Specially trained, nonattorney Notaries certified or licensed in a particular field (e.g., real estate, insurance, escrow, etc.) may offer advice or prepare documents related to that field only. Paralegals under the supervision of an attorney may give advice about documents in routine legal matters.

Do Not Solicit for Attorney. According to the New York Department of State, a Notary may not refer legal matters to a lawyer, nor may the Notary receive any compensation for doing so. A Notary is strictly prohibited from dividing fees with a lawyer, or accepting any part of a lawyer's fee for any legal business. (NPLL, "Professional Conduct")

Signature by Mark

Mark Serves as Signature. A person who cannot sign his or her name because of illiteracy or a physical disability may instead use a mark — an "X", for example — as a signature, as long as there are two witnesses to the making of the mark.

Witnesses. For a signature by mark to be notarized, the National Notary Association recommends that there be two witnesses to the making of the mark *in addition to the Notary.*
Both witnesses should sign the document and the Notary's journal if one is being kept. One witness should legibly print the marker's name in the journal and beside the mark on the document. It is recommended that a mark also be affixed in the Notary's journal.

Notarization Procedures. Because a properly witnessed mark is considered a signature under custom and law, no special notarial certificate is required. As required of any other signer, the marker must be positively identified.

Notarizing for Minors

Under Age 18. Generally, persons must reach the age of majority before they can handle their own legal affairs and sign documents for themselves. In New York, the age of majority is 18. Normally, natural guardians (parents) or court-appointed guardians will sign on a minor's behalf. In certain cases, where minors are engaged in business transactions or serving as court witnesses, they may lawfully sign documents and have their signatures notarized.

Include Age Next to Signature. When notarizing for a minor, the Notary should ask the young signer to write his or her age next to the signature to alert any person relying on the document that the signer is a minor. The Notary is not required to verify the minor signer's age.

Identification. The method for identifying a minor is the same as that for an adult. However, determining the identity of a minor can be a problem because minors often do not possess acceptable identification documents such as driver's licenses or passports. If the minor does not have an acceptable ID, then the other methods of identifying acknowledgers must be used, either the Notary's personal knowledge of the minor or the oath of a credible identifying witness who can identify the minor. See "Credible Identifying Witness(es)," pages 39–40.

Authentication

Documents Sent Out of State. Documents notarized in New York State and sent to other states and nations may be required to bear proof that the Notary's signature and seal are genuine and that the Notary had authority to act at the time of notarization. This process of proving the genuineness of an official signature and seal is called *authentication* or *legalization*.

In New York State, the proof is in the form of an authenticating certificate attached to the notarized document by either the Department of State or by the County Clerk's office where the Notary's signature and certificate of official character are filed.

These authentication certificates are known by different names: certificates of authority, certificates of capacity, certificates of authenticity, certificates of prothonotary and "flags."

The County Clerk may charge a $3 fee for issuing a certificate of authentication for attachment to a notarized document. Any New York Notary may file a signature sample and certificate of official character in any additional counties in the state, thus permitting these counties to issue authentication certificates for that Notary. A county will charge the Notary $10 for filing a certificate of official character in an additional county. (Executive Law, Sections 132, 133)

In sending a notarized document from New York to another U.S. state or territory, an attached certificate from the County Clerk is normally sufficient authentication. However, if an authentication certificate from the New York Department of State is necessary in addition to the County Clerk's authentication certificate, the New York Department of State may charge $10.

The New York Department of State issues authenticating certificates at two locations:

Department of State
Miscellaneous Records
41 State Street
Albany, NY 12231
1-518-474-4770

Department of State
Certification Unit
270 Broadway, Room 620
New York, NY 10007
1-212-417-5687

<u>Documents Sent Out of Country</u>. If the notarized document is going out of the United States, a chain authentication process may be necessary. Additional certificates of authority may have to be obtained from the U.S. Department of State in Washington, D.C., a foreign consulate in Washington, D.C. and a ministry of foreign affairs in the particular foreign nation.

<u>*Apostilles* and the Hague Convention</u>. Fortunately, over 60 nations, including the United States, subscribe to a treaty under auspices of the Hague Conference that simplifies authentication of notarized documents exchanged between any of these nations. The official name of this treaty, adopted by the Conference on October 5, 1961, is the Hague Convention Abolishing the Requirement of Legalization for Foreign Public Documents. For a list of the subscribing countries, see "Hague Convention Nations," pages 113–115.

Under the Hague Convention, only one authenticating certificate called an *apostille* is necessary to ensure acceptance in these subscribing countries. (*Apostille* is French for "notation".)

In New York, *apostilles* are issued by the Department of State's office (listed above) for a $10 fee per notarized document. Unfortunately, New York also requires the notarized document to bear an authenticating certificate from the County Clerk before issuing an *apostille*. In most other states, the *apostille* is the only authenticating form required.

An *apostille* must be specifically requested in writing, including the name, address and telephone number of the person making the request. The letter must also identify the nation to which the document will be sent. A person requesting the apostille should send the letter, the notarized document bearing the county's authenticating certificate and the $10 fee per notarized document (payable to the "New York State Department of State") to one of the Department of State offices listed above.

It is *not* the Notary's responsibility to obtain an *apostille*, but rather, it is the responsibility of the party sending the document.

Advertising

False or Misleading Advertising. A Notary's commission may be revoked or suspended if the Notary advertises or claims to have powers not authorized by law. For example, a Notary may not claim to have authority to officially certify the translation of a document, since this is not a power given by New York law.

For practicing fraud or deceit in advertising or in any other activity as a Notary, the Notary may be found guilty of a misdemeanor and removed from office. For a Class A misdemeanor, a prison term of up to one year may be imposed. (Executive Law, Section 135-a and NPLL, "Professional Conduct")

Foreign Languages

Foreign-Language Documents. New York Notaries are not prohibited from notarizing a non-English document as long as the certificate and document signature are in English or in a language the Notary can read.

However, any document conveying title to real estate that is presented for recording in a county office must be completely in English, including the Notary's certificate and any authenticating certificates. Proper names may be in a foreign language, as long as the letters used are those of the English language. A non-English-language conveyance may only be recorded in New York State if accompanied by a duly certified English-language translation. (Real Property Law, Section 333)

There are difficulties to consider with foreign-language documents: blatant fraud might be undetectable; the Notary seal might be misinterpreted in another country; and making a journal entry may be difficult.

If the Notary encounters difficulty with a foreign-language document, the signer could be referred to a Notary who can read the language; in large cities, such multilingual Notaries are often found in ethnic neighborhoods or in foreign consulates.

If a Notary chooses to notarize a document that he or she cannot read, at the very least the notarial certificate should be in English, or in a language the Notary can read, and the signature notarized should be written in characters that the Notary is familiar with.

Foreign-Speaking Signers. There should always be direct communication between the Notary and document signer —

whether in English or any other language. The Notary should never rely on an intermediary or interpreter to determine a signer's willingness or competence. A third party may have a motive for misrepresenting the circumstances to the Notary and/or to the signer.

Immigration Documents

Do Not Give Advice. Nonattorney Notaries may never advise others on the subject of immigration, nor help others prepare immigration documents — especially not for a fee. Under New York statute, Notaries who offer immigration advice to others may be prosecuted for the unauthorized practice of law. (Judiciary Law, Section 484)

Common Documents. Affidavits are the forms issued or accepted by the U.S. Immigration and Naturalization Service (INS) that are most often notarized, with the "Affidavit of Support" (Form I-134) being the most common.

Non-INS-issued documents are often notarized and submitted in support of an immigration petition. These may include translator's declarations, statements from employers and banks, and affidavits of relationship.

Naturalization Certificates. It can be a serious violation of federal law for a Notary to make a typewritten, photostatic or any other copy of a certificate of naturalization or notarize it. Severe penalties are prescribed, including imprisonment. (U.S. Penal Code, Section 75 and U.S. Code, Title 18, Section 137)

Military-Officer Notarizations

May Notarize Worldwide. Certain U.S. military officers may notarize for military personnel and their dependents anywhere in the world. Under statutory authority, the following persons are authorized to act as Notaries:

• Civilian attorneys employed as legal assistance attorneys and licensed to practice law in the United States.

• Judge advocates on active duty or training as reservists on inactive duty.

• All adjutants, assistant adjutants, acting adjutants and

personnel adjutants.

• Enlisted paralegals, personnel rank E-4 or higher, on active duty or training on inactive duty.

• Active duty personnel who are commissioned officers or senior noncommissioned officers (rank E-7 or higher) who are stationed at a Geographically Separated Unit (GSU) or location where no authorized Notary official is available, and who are appointed in writing by the unit's servicing general courtmartial convening authority.

Certificate. When signing documents in their official capacity, military-officer Notaries must specify the date and location of the notarization, list their title and office, and use a raised seal or inked stamp citing Title 10 U.S.C. 1044a. (U.S. Code, Title 10, Sections 936, 1044a)

In addition, New York law stipulates that a military-officer notarization may only be performed for a person on active duty, for a dependent of a person on active duty or for a person officially accompanying the armed forces. The certificate must also state the rank, serial number and command of the person taking the acknowledgment, as well as the serial number, if any, of the person making the acknowledgment. (Real Property Law, Section 300)

Authentication. Authentication of a military-officer notarization certificate is not required. (Real Property Law, Section 300)

Wills

Do Not Offer Advice. A Notary risks prosecution for the unauthorized practice of law in advising a signer how to proceed with a will. Ill-informed advice may adversely affect the affairs of the signer. The format of a will is dictated by strict laws, and any deviation may result in nullification. In some cases, holographic (handwritten) wills have actually been voided by notarization. (NPLL, "Professional Conduct" and "Restrictions and Violations")

Signatures of Witnesses Notarized. In New York, self-proving wills may require the signatures of the witnesses to be notarized. A Notary should notarize signatures of witnesses on a document described as a will *only* if a notarial certificate is provided or stipulated for each signer and the signers are not asking questions about how to proceed. Any such questions should be answered by an attorney. (NPLL, "Professional Conduct")

The New York Department of State warns Notaries not to execute an acknowledgment certificate when asked to notarize a will: "Such acknowledgment cannot be deemed equivalent to an attestation clause accompanying a will." (The attestation clause is the statement at the end of the will wherein the witnesses certify that the document was executed before them.) (NPLL, "Professional Conduct," "Restrictions and Violations")

Living Wills. Documents popularly called "living wills" may be notarized. These are not actual wills, but written statements of a signer's wishes concerning medical treatment in the event he or she is unable to issue instructions on his or her own behalf.

Certificate Provided. A Notary should notarize a document described as a will *only* if a notarial certificate is provided or stipulated for each signer and the signers are not asking questions about how to proceed. Any such questions should be answered by an attorney. (NPLL, "Professional Conduct")

Digital Signatures

No Notarization Procedures Established. Notaries should *not* attempt to notarize digital signatures. As yet, there are no procedures for doing so. In addition, the use of a digital or computer-made Notary signature is not allowed by law.

MISCONDUCT, FINES AND PENALTIES

Misconduct

Misconduct Defined. In New York, a Notary (or any other public servant) is guilty of "official misconduct" when with intent to deceive another person to obtain a benefit, the Notary:

1) Knowingly performs a notarial act, or an act related to the function of the Notary, in an unauthorized manner; or

2) Knowingly refuses to perform a notarial act without due cause.

Official misconduct by a Notary is a Class A Misdemeanor,

which is punishable by a prison term of up to one year. (Penal Law, Sections 70.15, 195.00)

Misconduct by Notary. For any act of official misconduct by a Notary, the New York Secretary of State may suspend the commission of the Notary — meaning, the commission will not be taken away, but it cannot currently be used.

For misconduct, the Secretary of State also has the option of removing the Notary from office or imposing a fine. None of these three penalties may be imposed, however, without first giving the accused Notary the chance to respond to the charges. (Executive Law, Section 130)

In addition, a Notary Public is liable for any damages to parties injured, and criminal and civil lawsuits against the Notary may result from an act of misconduct. (Executive Law, Section 135)

Application Misstatement. Substantial and material misstatement or omission in the application for a Notary commission is reason for the Secretary of State to revoke, suspend or refuse to grant a Notary's commission. (Executive Law, Section 135-a, NPLL, "Restrictions and Violations")

Felony Conviction. Conviction for a felony or any offense involving moral depravity — such as engaging in prostitution or vagrancy, or possessing or distributing drugs — or of a nature incompatible with notarial duties, such as a forgery conviction, is reason for the Secretary of State to revoke, suspend or refuse to grant a Notary's commission. (Executive Law, Section 130, Penal Law, Section 170.10)

Falsely Acting as a Notary. Any person who is not a Notary and who represents himself or herself as a Notary Public is guilty of a misdemeanor. (Executive Law, Section 135-a)

A Notary who acts as a Notary before taking the oath of office is guilty of a misdemeanor. (NPLL, "Restrictions and Violations")

Must Affix Statement. A Notary must print, typewrite or stamp in black ink the following information to each instrument: the Notary's name; the words "Notary Public State of New York"; the name of the county in which the Notary has originally qualified; the Notary's commission expiration date;

and the name of any county in which the Notary has filed a certificate of official character, stated as "Certificate filed _____ County."

Failure to include such information may subject the Notary to disciplinary action by the Secretary of State. (Executive Law, Section 137)

Making False Statements to Notary. A person is guilty of perjury if he or she has stated or given testimony, under oath or affirmation, as to the truth of a document when he or she knew the statement was false. The Notary will be subject to removal from office for administering an oath the Notary knows to be false. (NPLL, "Definitions," "Miscellaneous," "Restrictions and Violations")

False or Misleading Advertising. The use of false or misleading advertising by a Notary to represent that he or she has duties, rights and privileges not given by law is reason for the Secretary of State to remove the Notary from office and subjects the Notary to possible imprisonment, fine, or both. (Executive Law, Section 135-a, NPLL, "Professional Conduct")

Immigration Advice. A Notary may not claim to be an immigration expert or counselor nor help others prepare immigration documents. Under New York statute, Notaries who offer immigration advice to others may be prosecuted for the unauthorized practice of law. (Judiciary Law, Section 484)

Unauthorized Practice of Law. The unauthorized practice of law, such as giving advice about a legal document when one is not a lawyer, is reason for removal from office by the Secretary of State, imprisonment, fine or both. A Notary may not: give advice on the law; ask for and receive legal business, for money or other consideration; send business to a lawyer; divide or agree to divide notarial fees with a lawyer or accept any portion of a lawyer's fee for any legal business; or advertise that the Notary has powers not duly granted. (NPLL, "Professional Conduct")

In addition to penalties imposed by the Secretary of State, the Supreme Court has the power to prosecute for criminal contempt any person who unlawfully practices or assumes to practice law. (Judiciary Law, Section 750)

A Notary cannot counsel or advise on the drawing of agreements, the organization of corporations and preparing such papers, or draft legal documents of any kind, including wills. (Judiciary Law, Section 484)

A Notary Public engaged in the unauthorized practice of law may be guilty of a misdemeanor. (Judiciary Law, Section 485)

Representing Corporation — Financial Interest. A Notary who is a stockholder, director, officer or employee of a corporation may take an acknowledgment or proof of any person in the corporation who is executing a corporate instrument, and the Notary may protest for nonpayment that instrument. However, a Notary may not notarize if the Notary is a party executing the instrument and may financially benefit from the transaction. (Executive Law, Section 138)

Overcharging. A Notary who charges more than the legally prescribed fees is subject to removal from office and criminal or civil penalties, including criminal prosecution and civil action in which the person overcharged may seek triple the damages. (Public Officers Law, Section 67)

Dishonesty or Fraud. Commission of an act involving dishonesty, fraud, or deceit with the intent to substantially benefit the Notary or another, or substantially injure another, is included in the definition of "official misconduct." Such misconduct is a Class A Misdemeanor, which is punishable by a prison term of up to one year. (Penal Law, Sections 70.15, 195.00)

False Acknowledgments. A Notary must ensure that a certificate for an acknowledgment reflects the date the signer actually appeared before the Notary. A certificate that indicates a different date than when the signer actually appeared may be fraudulent. (NPLL, "Definitions and Terms")

An injured party may recover damages against the Notary who issues a false acknowledgment. The Notary may also be guilty of forgery in the second degree, a Class D Felony, which is punishable by a prison term of up to seven years. (Penal Law, Sections 70.00, 170.10)

Telephone Acknowledgments. Any Notary who engages in taking acknowledgments — or administering oaths or

affirmations over the telephone — without the personal
appearance of the signer is guilty of a misdemeanor. (NPLL,
"Professional Conduct" and "Definitions and General Terms")

False Certificate. A Notary who completes a false certificate is
subject to a felony conviction when the Notary knowingly makes
the certificate with intent to defraud, or when the Notary
completes the certificate when he or she knows that it contains
false information. (Penal Law, Section 175.40)

A Notary who knowingly completes a false notarial
certificate may be guilty of a Class D Felony, punishable by a
prison term of up to seven years, or a Class E Felony, for
which a prison term of up to four years may be imposed.
(Penal Law, Sections 70, 170.10, 175.40, NPLL, "Definitions and
General Terms")

False Acknowledgment on Conveyance. A Notary may not
take an acknowledgment unless the Notary has satisfactory
evidence that the person making the acknowledgment is the
same person that is described in the document. (Real Property
Law, Section 303)

A Notary who executes a fraudulent acknowledgment of a
conveyance of real property will be held liable for damages to
any person injured. If, for example, a lender accepts a forged,
notarized deed as collateral for a loan, the lender might sue the
Notary who witnesses the bogus deed to recover losses. (Real
Property Law, Section 330)

Unauthorized Certified Copies. A New York Notary is not
authorized to issue certified copies. A Notary who makes and
issues a certified copy and collects a fee for doing so may
receive an official warning from the Secretary of State. After a
Notary has received an official warning, a subsequent action will
be considered to be official misconduct, and the Notary will be
removed from office. (NPLL, "Definitions")

Naturalization Certificate Copies or Notarizations. A Notary
may be in violation of federal law if he or she makes a
typewritten, photostatic or any other copy of a certificate of
naturalization or notarizes it. (U.S. Penal Code, Section 75 and
U.S.Code, Title 18, Section 137)

Oath or Affirmation Not Administered. Notaries must administer oaths and affirmations in specific forms and as required by law. A Notary may be charged with a Class A Misdemeanor if he or she refuses to perform a duty imposed by law. (Penal Law, Section 195.00)

Civil Lawsuit

Liability for Damages. For any misconduct by a Notary in performing official duties, the Notary is liable for all damages to any person injured. (Executive Law, Section 135)

Right to Respond to Charges

Revocation, Suspension or Denial. Before the Secretary of State can suspend or revoke a commission due to professional misconduct, the accused Notary will have the chance to respond to the charges in a hearing. (Executive Law, Section 130) ■

Test Your Knowledge

Trial Exam

Instructions. This examination is designed to test your knowledge of the basic concepts of notarization. It will also help you prepare for the proctored New York Notary Public exam that you must pass before being commissioned as a New York Notary. The questions here, of course, are not the same as those on the official test. Also, the Notary Public exam is made up of multiple-choice questions, with no true/false or essay questions as in this trial exam.

Work through this exam without looking at the answers, then check your responses and note where you need additional study. Careful review of "Notary Laws Explained" (pages 17–66), the reprinted Notary statutes (pages 73–103), "10 Most-Asked Questions" (pages 8–12) and "Steps to Proper Notarization" (pages 13–16) will produce the answers.

Scoring. A perfect score on this examination is 100 points. There are:

- 20 true/false questions worth 1 point each
- 5 multiple-choice questions worth 4 points each
- 5 fill-in-the-blank questions worth 4 points each
- 5 essay questions worth 8 points each.

Now, get a separate sheet of paper and a pen or pencil, and get ready to test your knowledge.

Part 1: True/False. For the following statements, answer true or false. Each correct answer is worth 1 point:

1. Notaries may act only in the county where they are commissioned. True or false?

2. The maximum Notary fee for taking the acknowledgment of two signers is $2. True or false?

3. Oaths and affirmations have the same legal effect. True or false?

4. Protests are one of the most common forms of notarization. True or false?

5. Notaries are obligated to ensure the truthfulness of the statements in the documents they notarize. True or false?

6. It is the duty of the Notary to decide what type of notarization is appropriate for a given document. True or false?

7. Though not legally required in New York State, use of a Notary seal and journal is a good practice. True or false?

8. A subscribing witness must sign the document in addition to the principal signer. True or false?

9. An employee of a corporation may notarize for the officers and stockholders of that corporation. True or false?

10. Notaries may use their own wills as models in advising clients about how to handle their estates. True or false?

11. An oath for a deposition may be given over the telephone. True or false?

12. An acknowledged document, such as a deed, must be signed in the Notary's presence. True or false?

13. A Social Security card and a birth certificate offer reliable proof of a document signer's identity. True or false?

14. An affiant must do more than merely nod in assent to an oath. True or false?

15. The letters "SS." indicate that Notaries must write in their Social Security numbers. True or false?

16. Certifying a copy is not an official notarial act in New York. True or false?

17. It is ill-advised to notarize a document whose blank spaces will be filled in later. True or false?

18. On a notarial certificate, the venue indicates where the Notary's oath has been filed. True or false?

19. Although technically different, the terms "affiant" and "deponent" are sometimes interchanged. True or false?

20. Notaries may not perform acknowledgements on Sunday. True or false?

Multiple Choice. Choose the one best answer to each question. Each correct answer is worth 4 points.

1. In executing an acknowledgment, a Notary certifies that...
   a. the signer took an oath or affirmation.
   b. the signer was positively identified by the Notary.
   c. the signer signed in the Notary's presence.

2. In executing a jurat, a Notary certifies that...
   a. the signer was positively identified by the Notary.
   b. the signer was given an oath by the Notary.
   c. the signer has no direct interest in the document.

3. Non-English-language real property deeds...
   a. cannot be notarized in New York.
   b. are illegal in New York.
   c. cannot be recorded in New York without a translation.

4. Notaries may be liable...
   a. only for their intentional acts.
   b. only for damages suffered by the signer.
   c. for all damages caused by their misconduct

5. It could be the unauthorized practice of law to...

a. explain a paragraph in an immigration document.
b. provide a notarial certificate requested by the signer.
c. type a paper following the signer's instructions.

Fill in the Blank. Write in the word or phrase that best completes each sentence. Each correct answer is worth 4 points.

1. A _____ must often be attached to a notarized document sent out of state.

2. An affirmation is a solemn, spoken pledge that does not refer to a _____.

3. The best ID cards contain the following three elements:
a) _____; b) _____; and c) _____.

4. Without ID cards or personal knowledge of a signer's identity, Notaries may rely on the oath of a _____ to identify the stranger.

5. The state official who appoints and regulates New York Notaries is the _____.

Essay. Reply to each question or statement with a short paragraph. Each complete and correct response is worth 8 points.

1. Under what conditions should a Notary execute a protest?

2. Why do most Notaries never execute depositions?

3. Why is a Social Security card all but worthless as an ID?

4. May Notaries notarize for relatives?

5. Outline the differences between an acknowledgment certificate and a jurat.

Test Answers

True/False. 1. F; 2. F; 3 T; 4. F; 5 F; 6. F; 7. T; 8. T; 9. T; 10. F; 11. F; 12. F; 13. F; 14. T; 15. F; 16. T ; 17. T; 18. F; 19. T; 20. F

Multiple Choice. 1. b; 2. b; 3. c; 4. c; 5. a

Fill In The Blank. 1. certificate of authentication; 2. Supreme Being; 3. photograph, signature and physical description; 4. credible identifying witness; 5. Secretary of State

Essay. Responses should include the basic information in the paragraphs below:

1. Since protests are complicated notarial acts, Notaries should only execute them if they understand the legal and financial terminology used in the protest certificate or if they are under the supervision of a person with such an understanding.

2. Depositions are normally executed by professional shorthand reporters who are able to readily transcribe oral testimony. Also, because strict rules of procedure dictate how depositions are executed, Notaries without appropriate training or supervision should not attempt them.

3. A Social Security card is very easily counterfeited and has only one of the three vital elements of a good ID: a signature. Reliable IDs also bear a photograph and a physical description.

4. Although New York law does not specifically prohibit notarizing for family members, in so doing a Notary may violate restrictions against notarizing with a financial interest, especially in the case of spouses, parents and children. Notaries should fully live up to their roles as impartial witnesses and never notarize for close relatives.

5. An acknowledgment certificate certifies that the signer of the document personally appeared before the Notary on the date and in the county indicated. It also certifies that the signer's identity was satisfactorily proven to the Notary and that the signer acknowledged having signed freely. A jurat certifies that the signer personally appeared before the Notary on the date and in the county indicated, that an oath or affirmation was administered to the signer by the Notary, and that, in most cases, the document was signed in the Notary's presence.

Tally Your Score

After checking your answers, add up your score. Then look at the grading scale below to determine how you stand:

- 90–100: Excellent!
- 80–89: Good, but some review needed.
- 70–79: Fair. Reread the parts of the *Primer* covering the answers you missed.
- Below 70: Below par. Study the laws again thoroughly. ∎

New York Laws Pertaining to Notaries Public

Reprinted on the following pages are pertinent sections of the New York *Notary Public License Law*, sheets distributed to newly-commissioned Notaries by the New York Department of State.

This official information contains sections of New York statutes affecting Notaries and notarial acts, mostly drawn from the Executive Law, Judiciary Law, Penal Law, Public Officers Law and Real Property Law.

It also contains helpful instructions on notarial matters not contained in the statutes.

NOTARY PUBLIC LICENSE LAW

State of New York
Department of State
Division of Licensing Services

INTRODUCTION

Notaries are commissioned by the Secretary of State after they pass the walk-in examination and their applications are reviewed. The written examination is based on material contained in this booklet and may also include questions pertaining to general knowledge and reasoning ability.

Upon request, county clerks will authenticate the signature of the notary on a document and will attest to the notary's authority to sign. This is normally obtained when the document will be used outside the State. Notaries who expect to sign documents regularly in counties other than that of their residence may elect to file a certificate of official character with other New York State county clerks.

Out-of-State Residents. Attorneys, residing out of State, who are admitted to practice in the State and who maintain a law office within the State are deemed to be residents of the county where the office is maintained.

Nonresidents other than attorneys who have offices or places of business in New York State may also become notaries. The oath of office and signature of the notary must be filed in the office of the county clerk of the county in which the office or place of business is located.

PROFESSIONAL CONDUCT

Use of the office of notary in other than the specific, step-by-step procedure required is viewed as a serious offense by the Secretary of State. The practice of taking acknowledgements and affidavits over the telephone, or otherwise, without the actual, personal appearance of the individual making the acknowledgment or affidavit before the officiating notary, is illegal.

The attention of all notaries public is called to the following judicial declarations concerning such misconduct:

> "The court again wishes to express its condemnations of the acts of notaries taking acknowledgments or affidavits without the presence of the party whose acknowledgment is taken for the affiant, and that it will treat serious professional misconduct the act of any notary thus violating his official duty." (*Matter of Napolis*, 169 App. Div. 469, 472.)

> "Upon the faith of these acknowledgments rests the title of real property, and the only security to such titles is the fidelity with which notaries and commissioners of deeds perform their duty in requiring the appearance of parties to such instruments before them and always refusing to execute a certificate unless the parties are actually known to them or the identity of the parties executing the instruments is satisfactorily proved." (*Matter of Gottheim*, 153 App. Div. 779, 782.)

Equally unacceptable to the Secretary of State is slipshod administration of oaths. **The simplest form in which an oath may be lawfully administered is:**

> **"Do you solemnly swear that the contents of this affidavit subscribed by you is correct and true?"** (*Bookman v. City of New York*, 200 N.Y. 53, 56.)

Alternatively, the following affirmation may be used for persons who conscientiously decline taking an oath. This affirmation is legally equivalent to an oath and is just as binding:

> **"Do you solemnly, sincerely and truly declare and affirm that the statements made by you are true and correct?"**

"Whatever the form adopted, it must be in the presence of an officer authorized to administer it, and it must be an unequivocal and present act by which the affiant consciously takes upon himself the obligation of an oath." (Idem, citing People ex rel. *Kenyon v. Sutherland*, 81 N.Y. 1; *O'Reilly v. People*, 86 N.Y. 154, 158, 161.)

Unless a lawyer, the notary public may not engage directly or indirectly in the practice of law. Listed below are some of the activities involving the practice of law which are prohibited, and which subject the notary public to removal from office by the Secretary of State, and possible imprisonment, fine or both. A notary:

1. **May not give advice on the law.** The notary may not draw any kind of legal papers, such as wills, deeds, bills of sale, mortgages, chattel mortgages, contracts, leases, offers, options, incorporation papers, releases, mechanics liens, power of attorney, complaints and all legal pleadings, papers in summary proceedings to evict a tenant, or in bankruptcy, affidavits, or any papers which our courts have said are legal documents or papers.

2. **May not ask for and get legal** business to send to a lawyer or lawyers with whom he has any business connection or from whom he receives any money or other consideration for sending the business.

3. **May not divide or agree to divide** his fees with a lawyer or accept any part of a lawyer's fee on any legal business.

4. **May not advertise in, or circulate** in any manner, any paper or advertisement, or say to anyone that he has any powers or rights not given to the notary by the laws under which the notary was appointed.

A notary public is cautioned not to execute an acknowledgment of the execution of a will. Such acknowledgment cannot be deemed equivalent to an attestation clause accompanying a will. (*See definition of Attestation Clause*)

APPOINTMENT AND QUALIFICATIONS

Index

Public Officers Law	534	County Clerk; Appointment of Notaries
NYS Constitution	ART. II, SEC 7	Member of Legislature
NYS Constitution	ART. XIII, SEC 13a	Sheriffs
Miscellaneous		Disqualifications

Executive Law

§ 130. Appointment of notaries public.

The secretary of state may appoint and commission as many notaries public for the state of New York as in his judgment may be deemed best, whose jurisdiction shall be co-extensive with the boundaries of the state. The appointment of a notary public shall be for a term of 2 years. An application for an appointment as notary public shall be in form and set forth such matters as the secretary of state shall prescribe. Every person appointed as a notary public must, at the time of his appointment, be a citizen of the United States and either a resident of the state of New York or have an office or place of business in New York state. A notary public who is a resident of the state and who moves out of the state but still maintains a place of business or an office in New York state does not vacate his office as a notary public. A notary public who is a nonresident and who ceases to have an office or place of business in this state, vacates his office as a notary public. A notary public who is a resident of New York state and moves out of the state and who does not retain an office or place of business in this state shall vacate his office as a notary public. A non-resident who accepts the office of notary public in this state thereby appoints the secretary of state as the person upon whom process can be served on his behalf. Before issuing to any applicant a commission as notary public, unless he be an attorney and counsellor at law duly admitted to practice in this state, the secretary of state shall satisfy himself that the applicant is of good moral character, has the equivalent of a common school education and is familiar with the duties and responsibilities of a notary public; provided, however, that where a notary public applies, before the expiration of his term, for reappointment with the county clerk or where a person whose term as a notary public shall have expired applies within six months thereafter for reappointment as a notary public with the county clerk, such qualifying requirements may be waived by the secretary of state, and further, where an application for reappointment is filed with the county clerk after the expiration of the aforementioned renewal period by a person who failed or was unable to re-apply by reason of his induction or enlistment in the armed forces of the United States, such qualifying requirements may also be waived by the secretary of state, provided such application for reappointment is made within a period of one year after the military discharge of the applicant under conditions other than dishonorable. In any case, the appointment or reappointment of any applicant is in the discretion of the secretary of state. The secretary of state may suspend or remove from office, for misconduct, any notary public appointed by him but no such removal shall be made unless the person who is sought to be removed shall have been served with a copy of the charges against him and have an opportunity of being heard. No person shall be appointed as a notary public under this article who has been convicted, in this state or any other state or territory, of a felony or any of the following offenses, to wit:

(a) Illegally using, carrying or possessing a pistol or other dangerous weapon;

(b) making or possessing burglar's instruments;

(c) buying or receiving or criminally possessing stolen property;

(d) unlawful entry of a building;

(e) aiding escape from prison;

(f) unlawfully possessing or distributing habit forming narcotic drugs;

(g) violating sections 270, 270-a, 270-b, 270-c, 271, 275, 276, 550, 551, 551-a and subdivision 6, 8, 10 or 11 of section 722 of the former penal law as in force and effect immediately prior to September 1, 1967, or violating sections 165.25, 165.30, subdivision 1 of section 240.30, subdivision 3 of section 240.35 of the penal law, or violating sections 478, 479, 480, 481, 484, 489 and 491 of the judiciary law; or

(h) vagrancy or prostitution, and who has not subsequent to such conviction received an executive pardon therefor or a certificate of good conduct from the parole board to remove the disability under this section because of such conviction.

A person regularly admitted to practice as an attorney and counsellor in the courts of record of this state, whose office for the practice of law is within the state, may be appointed a notary public and retain his office as such notary public although he resides in or removes to an adjoining state. For the purpose of this and the following sections of this article such person shall be deemed a resident of the county where he maintains such office.

§ 131. Procedure of appointment; fees and commissions.
1. Applicants for a notary public commission shall submit to the secretary of state with their application the oath of office, duly executed before any person authorized to administer an oath, together with their signature.
2. Upon being satisfied of the competency and good character of applicants for appointment as notaries public, the secretary of state shall

issue a commission to such persons; and the official signature of the applicants and the oath of office filed with such applications shall take effect.

3. The secretary of state shall receive a non-refundable application fee of thirty dollars from applicants for appointment, which fee shall be submitted together with the application. No further fee shall be paid for the issuance of the commission.

4. A notary public identification card indicating the appointee's name, address, county and commission term shall be transmitted to the appointee.

5. The commission, duly dated, and a certified copy or the original of the oath of office and the official signature, and ten dollars apportioned from the application fee shall be transmitted by the secretary of state to the county clerk in which the appointee resides by the tenth day of the following month.

6. The county clerk shall make a proper index of commissions and official signatures transmitted to that office by the secretary of state pursuant to the provisions of this section.

7. Applicants for reappointment of a notary public commission shall submit to the county clerk with their application the oath of office, duly executed before any person authorized to administer an oath, together with their signature.

8. Upon being satisfied of the completeness of the application for reappointment, the county clerk shall issue a commission to such persons; and the official signature of the applicants and oath of office filed with such applications shall take effect.

9. The county clerk shall receive a non-refundable application fee of thirty dollars from each applicant for reappointment, which fee shall be submitted together with the application. No further fee shall be paid for the issuance of the commission.

10. The commission, duly dated, and a certified or original copy of the application, and twenty dollars apportioned from the application fee plus interest as may be required by statute shall be transmitted by the county clerk to the secretary of state by the tenth day of the following month.

11. The secretary of state shall make a proper record of commissions transmitted to that office by the county clerk pursuant to the provisions of this section.

12. Except for changes made in an application for reappointment, the secretary of state shall receive a non-refundable fee of ten dollars for changing the name or address of a notary public.

13. The secretary of state may issue a duplicate identification card to a notary public for one lost, destroyed or damaged upon application therefor on a form prescribed by the secretary of state and upon payment of a non-refundable fee of ten dollars. Each such duplicate identification card shall have the word "duplicate" stamped across the face thereof and shall bear the same number as the one it replaces.

§ 132. Certificates of official character of notaries public.

The secretary of state or the county clerk of the county in which the commission of a notary public is filed may certify to the official character of such notary public and any notary public may file his autograph signature and a certificate of official character in the office of any county clerk of any county in the state and in any register's office in any county having a register and thereafter such county clerk may certify as to the official character of such notary public. The secretary of state shall collect for each certificate of official character issued by him the sum of $10. The county clerk and register of any county with whom a certificate of official character has been filed shall collect for filing the same the sum of $10. For each certificate of official character issued, with seal attached, by any county clerk, the sum of $5 shall be collected by him.

§ 133. Certification of notarial signatures.

The county clerk of a county in whose office any notary public has qualified or has filed his autograph signature and a certificate of his official character, shall, when so requested and upon payment of a fee of $3 affix to any certificate of proof or acknowledgment or oath signed by such notary anywhere in the state of New York, a certificate under his hand and seal, stating that a commission or a certificate of his official character with his autograph signature has been filed in his office, and that he was at the time of taking such proof or acknowledgment or oath duly authorized to take the same; that he is well acquainted with the handwriting of such notary public or has compared the signature on the certificate of proof or acknowledgment or oath with the autograph signature deposited in his office by such notary public and believes that the signature is genuine. An instrument with such certificate of authentication of the county clerk affixed thereto shall be entitled to be read in evidence or to be recorded in any of the counties of this state in respect to which a certificate of a county clerk may be necessary for either purpose.

Executive Law — § 140[1]
[Commissioners of deeds in the city of New York.]

14. No person who has been removed from office as a commissioner of deeds for the city of New York, as hereinbefore provided, shall thereafter be eligible again to be appointed as such commissioner nor, shall he be eligible thereafter to appointment to the office of notary public.

15. Any person who has been removed from office as aforesaid, who shall, after knowledge of such removal, sign or execute any instrument as a commissioner of deeds or notary public shall be deemed guilty of a misdemeanor.

---

[1] Statutory language of this section is summarized and not reprinted verbatim.

Election Law — § 3-200 and § 3-400[2]

[§ 3-200. Boards of elections; creation, qualifications of commissioners, removal. § 3-400. Election inspectors and poll clerks; provision for.]

A commissioner of elections or inspector of elections is eligible for the office of notary public.

Public Officers Law

§ 3. Qualifications for holding office, provides that:

No person is eligible for the office of notary public who has been convicted of a violation of the selective draft act of the U.S. enacted May 18, 1917, or the acts amendatory or supplemental thereto, or of the federal selective training and service act of 1940 or the acts amendatory thereof or supplemental thereto.

§ 534. County clerk; appointment of notaries public.

Each county clerk shall designate from among the members of his or her staff at least one notary public to be available to notarize documents for the public in each county clerk's office during normal business hours free of charge. Each individual appointed by the county clerk to be a notary public pursuant to this section shall be exempt from the examination fee and application fee required by section one hundred thirty-one of the Executive Law.

MISCELLANEOUS

[Section 7, Art. III of the Constitution of the State of New York.] Member of legislature.

"If a member of the legislature be * * * appointed to any office, civil * * * under the government * * * the State of New York * * * his or her acceptance thereof shall vacate his or her seat in the legislature, providing, however, that a member of the legislature may be appointed * * * to any office in which he or she shall receive no compensation." (Section 7 of Article III of the Constitution of the State of New York.) A member of the legislature may be appointed a notary public in view of transfer of power of such appointment from the governor and senate to the secretary of state. (1927, Op. Atty. Gen. 97.)

[Section 13(a), Art. XIII of the Constitution of the State of New York.]

Sheriffs.

* * * Sheriffs shall hold no other office. * * * (Section 13(a) of Article XIII of the Constitution of the State of New York.)

Notary public — disqualifications.

Though a person may be eligible to hold the office of notary the

---

[2] Statutory language of these sections is summarized and not reprinted verbatim.

person may be disqualified to act in certain cases by reason of having an interest in the case. To state the rule broadly: if the notary is party to or directly and pecuniarily interested in the transaction, the person is not capable of acting in that case. For example, a notary who is a grantee or mortgagee in a conveyance or mortgage is disqualified to take the acknowledgment of the grantor or mortgagor; likewise, a notary who is a trustee in a deed of trust; and, of course, a notary who is the grantor could not take his own acknowledgment. A notary beneficially interested in the conveyance by way of being secured thereby is not competent to take the acknowledgment of the instrument. In New York the courts have held an acknowledgment taken by a person financially or beneficially interested in a party to a conveyance or instrument of which it is a part to be a nullity; and that the acknowledgment of an assignment of a mortgage before one of the assignees is a nullity; and that an acknowledgment by one of the incorporators of the other incorporators who signed a certificate was of no legal effect.

POWERS AND DUTIES

Index

Public Officers   10   Administering Oath of Public
                                            Officer

Executive Law

§ 134. Signature and seal of county clerk.

The signature and seal of a county clerk, upon a certificate of official
character of a notary public or the signature of a county clerk upon a
certificate of authentication of the signature and acts of a notary public or
commissioner of deeds, may be a facsimile, printed, stamped, photographed
or engraved thereon.

§ 135. Powers and duties; in general; of notaries public who are attorneys at law.

Every notary public duly qualified is hereby authorized and empowered
within and throughout the state to administer oaths and affirmations, to
take affidavits and depositions, to receive and certify acknowledgments or
proof of deeds, mortgages and powers of attorney and other instruments in
writing; to demand acceptance or payment of foreign and inland bills of
exchange, promissory notes and obligations in writing, and to protest the
same for nonacceptance or nonpayment, as the case may require, and, for
use in another jurisdiction, to exercise such other powers and duties as by
the laws of nations and according to commercial usage, or by the laws of
any other government or country may be exercised and performed by
notaries public, provided that when exercising such powers he shall set
forth the name of such other jurisdiction.

A notary public who is an attorney at law regularly admitted to practice
in this state may, in his discretion, administer an oath or affirmation to or
take the affidavit or acknowledgment of his client in respect of any matter,
claim, action or proceeding.

For any misconduct by a notary public in the performance of any of his
powers such notary public shall be liable to the parties injured for all
damages sustained by them. A notary public shall not, directly or indirectly,
demand or receive for the protest for the nonpayment of any note, or for
the nonacceptance or nonpayment of any bill of exchange, check or draft
and giving the requisite notices and certificates of such protest, including his
notarial seal, if affixed thereto, any greater fee or reward than 75¢ for such
protest, and 10¢ for each notice, not exceeding 5, on any bill or note. Every
notary public having a seal shall, except as otherwise provided, and when
requested, affix his seal to such protest free of expense.

§135-a. Notary public or commissioner of deeds; acting without appointment; fraud in office.

1. Any person who holds himself out to the public as being entitled
to act as a notary public or commissioner of deeds, or who assumes, uses or
advertises the title of notary public or commissioner of deeds, or equivalent
terms in any language, in such a manner as to convey the impression that

he is a notary public or commissioner of deeds without having first been appointed as notary public or commissioner of deeds, or

2. A notary public or commissioner of deeds, who in the exercise of the powers, or in the performance of the duties of such office shall practice any fraud or deceit, the punishment for which is not otherwise provided for by this act, shall be guilty of a misdemeanor.

§ 136. Notarial fees.

A notary public shall be entitled to the following fees:

1. For administering an oath or affirmation, and certifying the same when required, except where another fee is specifically prescribed by statute, $2.00.

2. For taking and certifying the acknowledgment or proof of execution of a written instrument, by one person, $2.00, and by each additional person, $2.00, for swearing such witness thereto, $2.00.

§ 137. Statement as to authority of notaries public.

In exercising his powers pursuant to this article, **a notary public, in addition to the venue of his act and his signature, shall print, typewrite, or stamp beneath his signature in black ink, his name, the words "Notary Public State of New York," the name of the county in which he originally qualified, and the date upon which his commission expires** and, in addition, wherever required, a notary public shall also include the name of any county in which his certificate of official character is filed, using the words "Certificate filed _____ County." A notary public who is duly licensed as an attorney and counsellor at law in this state may in his discretion, substitute the words "Attorney and Counsellor at Law" for the words "Notary Public." A notary public who has qualified or who has filed a certificate of official character in the office of the clerk in a county or counties within the city of New York must also affix to each instrument his official number or numbers in black ink, as given to him by the clerk or clerks of such county or counties at the time such notary qualified in such county or counties and, if the instrument is to be recorded in an office of the register of the city of New York in any county within such city and the notary has been given a number or numbers by such register or his predecessors in any county or counties, when his autographed signature and certificate are filed in such office or offices pursuant to this chapter, he shall also affix such number or numbers. No official act of such notary public shall be held invalid on account of the failure to comply with these provisions. If any notary public shall wilfully fail to comply with any of the provisions of this section, he shall be subject to disciplinary action by the secretary of state. In all the courts within this state the certificate of a notary public, over his signature, shall be received as presumptive evidence of the facts contained in such certificate; provided, that any person interested as a party to a suit may contradict, by other evidence, the certificate of a notary public.

§ 138. Powers of notaries public or other officers who are stockholders, directors, officers or employees of a corporation.

A notary public, justice of the supreme court, a judge, clerk, deputy clerk, or special deputy clerk of a court, an official examiner of title, or the mayor or recorder of a city, a justice of the peace, surrogate, special surrogate, special county judge, or commissioner of deeds, who is a stockholder, director, officer or employee of a corporation may take the acknowledgment or proof of any party to a written instrument executed to or by such corporation, or administer an oath of any other stockholder, director, officer, employee or agent of such corporation, and such notary public may protest for nonacceptance or nonpayment, bills of exchange, drafts, checks, notes and other negotiable instruments owned or held for collection by such corporation; but none of the officers above named shall take the acknowledgement or proof of a written instrument by or to a corporation of which he is stockholder, director, officer or employee, if such officer taking such acknowledgment or proof to be a party executing such instrument, either individually or as representative of such corporation, nor shall a notary public protest any negotiable instruments owned or held for collection by such corporation, if such notary public be individually a party to such instrument, or have a financial interest in the subject of same. All such acknowledgments or proofs of deeds, mortgages or other written instruments, relating to real property heretofore taken before any of the officers afore said are confirmed. This act shall not affect any action or legal proceeding now pending.

§ 142-a. Validity of acts of notaries public and commissioners of deeds notwithstanding certain defects.

1. Except as provided in subdivision three of this section, the official certificates and other acts heretofore or hereafter made or performed of notaries public and commissioners of deeds heretofore or hereafter and prior to the time of their acts appointed or commissioned as such shall not be deemed invalid, impaired or in any manner defective, so far as they may be affected, impaired or questioned by reason of defects described in subdivision two of this section.

2. This section shall apply to the following defects:

(a) ineligibility of the notary public or commissioner of deeds to be appointed or commissioned as such;

(b) misnomer or misspelling of name or other error made in his appointment or commission;

(c) omission of the notary public or commissioner of deeds to take or file his official oath or otherwise qualify;

(d) expiration of his term, commission or appointment;

(e) vacating of his office by change of his residence, by acceptance of another public office, or by other action on his part;

(f) the fact that the action was taken outside the jurisdiction where the notary was public or commissioner of deeds was authorized to act.

3. No person shall be entitled to assert the effect of this section to overcome a defect or if the defect was apparent on the face of the certificate of the notary public or commissioner of deeds; provided however, that this subdivision shall not apply after the expiration of six months from the date of the act of the notary public or commissioner of deeds.

4. After the expiration of six months from the date of the official certificate or other act of the commissioner of deeds, subdivision one of this section shall be applicable to a defect consisting in omission of the certificate of a commissioner of deeds to state the date on which and the place in which an act was done, or consisting of an error in such statement.

5. This section does not relieve any notary public or commissioner of deeds from criminal liability imposed by reason of his act, or enlarge the actual authority of any such officer, nor limit any other statute or rule of law by reason of which the act of a notary public or commissioner of deeds, or the record thereof, is valid or is deemed valid in any case.

Real Property Law
§ 290. Definitions; effect of article.
* * * 3. The term "conveyance" includes every written instrument, by which any estate or interest in real property is created, transferred, mortgaged or assigned, or by which the title to any real property may be affected, including an instrument in execution of power, although the power be one of revocation only, and an instrument postponing or subordinating a mortgage lien; except a will, a lease for a term not exceeding three years, an executory contract for the sale or purchase of lands, and an instrument containing a power to convey real property as the agent or attorney for the owner of such property.

§ 298. Acknowledgments and proofs within the state.
The acknowledgment or proof, within this state, of a conveyance of real property situate in this state may be made:

1. At any place within the state, before (a) a justice of the supreme court; (b) an official examiner of title; (c) an official referee; or (d) a notary public.

2. Within the district wherein such officer is authorized to perform official duties, before (a) a judge or clerk of any court of record; (b) a commissioner of deeds outside of the city of New York, or a commissioner of deeds of the city of New York within the five counties comprising the city of New York; (c) the mayor or recorder of a city; (d) a surrogate, special surrogate, or special county judge; or (e) the county clerk or other recording officer of a county.

3. Before a justice of the peace, town councilman, village police justice or a judge of any court of inferior local jurisdiction, anywhere within the county containing the town, village or city in which he is authorized to perform official duties.

§ 302. Acknowledgments and proofs by married women.

The acknowledgment or proof of a conveyance of real property, within the state, or of any other written instrument, may be made by a married woman the same if unmarried.

§ 303. Requisites of acknowledgments.

An acknowledgment must not be taken by any officer unless he knows or has satisfactory evidence, that the person making it is the person described in and who executed such instrument.

§ 304. Proof by subscribing witness.

When the execution of a conveyance is proved by a subscribing witness, such witness must state his own place of residence, and if his place of residence is in a city, the street and street number, if any thereof, and that he knew the person described in and who executed the conveyance. The proof must not be taken unless the officer is personally acquainted with such witness, or has satisfactory evidence that he is the same person, who was a subscribing witness to the conveyance.

§ 306. Certificate of acknowledgment or proof.

A person taking the acknowledgment or proof of a conveyance must endorse thereupon or attach thereto, a certificate, signed by himself, stating all the matters required to be done, known, or proved on the taking of such acknowledgment or proof; together with the name and substance of the testimony of each witness examined before him, and if a subscribing witness, his place of residence.* * *

§ 309. Acknowledgment by corporation and form of certificate.

1. The acknowledgment of a conveyance or other instrument by a corporation, must be made by an officer or attorney in fact duly appointed, or in case of a dissolved corporation, by an officer, director or attorney in fact duly appointed thereof authorized to execute the same by the board of directors of said corporation.

2. The certificate of acknowledgment must conform substantially with one of the following alternative forms, the blanks being properly filled:

State of New York   ) ss.:
County of _____)

On the _____ day of _____ in the year _____ before me personally came _____ to me known, who, being by me duly sworn, did depose and say that he/she/they reside(s) in _____ (if the place of residence is in a city, include the street and street number, if any, thereof); that he/she/they is (are) the (president or other officer or director or attorney in fact duly appointed) of the (name of corporation), the corporation described in and which executed the above instrument; that he/she/they know(s) the seal of said corporation; the seal affixed to said instrument is such corporate seal; that it was so affixed by authority of the board of directors of said corporation, and that he/she/they signed his/her/their name(s) thereto by like authority.

(Signature and office of person taking acknowledgment.)

State of New York) ss.:
County of _____)

On the _____ day of _____ in the year _____ before me personally came _____ to me known, who, being by me duly sworn, did depose and say that he/she/they reside(s) in _____ (if the place of residence is in a city, include the street and street number, if any, thereof); that he/she/they is (are) the (president or other officer or director or attorney in fact duly appointed) of the (name of corporation), the corporation described in and which executed the above instrument; and that he/she/they signed his/her/their name(s) thereto by authority of the board of directors of said corporation.

(Signature and office of person taking acknowledgment.)

[3] (3. Subdivision two of this section shall be inapplicable to the acknowledgment, within this state, of a conveyance or other instrument in respect to real property situate in this state executed on or after the first day of September, nineteen hundred ninety-nine. A certificate of such an acknowledgment shall be subject to the provisions of sections three hundred nine-a of this article.)

§ 330. Officers guilty of malfeasance liable for damages.
An officer authorized to take the acknowledgment or proof of a conveyance or other instrument, or to certify such proof or acknowledgment, or to record the same, who is guilty of malfeasance or fraudulent practice in the execution of any duty prescribed by law in relation thereto, is liable in damages to the person injured.

§ 333. When conveyances of real property not to be recorded.
* * * 2. A recording officer shall not record or accept for record any conveyance of real property, unless said conveyance in its entirety and the certificate of acknowledgment or proof and the authentication thereof, other

[3] Real Property section 309 has been amended by Chapter 179 of the 1997 Laws of New York, which added this subdivision 3 and replaced "he" in the two corporate certificates with "he/she/they," as also reflected above. The certificates set out in this section 309 will be valid until September 1, 1999, at which time they will be replaced by the certificates set out in Real Property section 309-a. See pages 102–103 for the text of Real Property section 309-a.

than proper names therein which may be in another language provided they are written in English letters or characters, shall be in the English language, or unless such conveyance, certificate of acknowledgment or proof, and the authentication thereof be accompanied by and have attached thereto a translation in the English language duly executed and acknowledged by the person or persons making such conveyance and proved and authenticated, if need be, in the manner required of conveyances for recording in this state, or, unless such conveyance, certificate of acknowledgment or proof, and the authentication thereof be accompanied by and have attached thereto a translation in the English language made by a person duly designated for such purpose by the county judge of the county where it is desired to record such conveyance or a justice of the supreme court and be duly signed, acknowledged and certified under oath or upon affirmation by such person before such a judge, to be a true and accurate translation and contain a certification of the designation of such person by such judge.

Special Note

By reason of changes in certain provisions of the Real Property Law, any and all limitations on the authority of a notary public to act as such in any part of the State have been removed; a notary public may now, in addition to administering oaths or taking affidavits anywhere in the State, take acknowledgments and proofs of conveyances anywhere in the State. The need for a certificate of authentication of a county clerk as a prerequisite to recording or use in evidence in this State of the instrument acknowledged or proved has been abolished. The certificate of authentication may possibly be required where the instrument is to be recorded or used in evidence outside the jurisdiction of the State.

Banking Law — § 335[4]

[Special remedies where rental of safe deposit box is not paid or when safe deposit box is not vacated on termination of lease.]

If the rental fee of any safe deposit box is not paid, or after the termination of the lease for such box, and at least 30 days after giving proper notice to the lessee, the lessor (bank) may, in the presence of a notary public, open the safe deposit box, remove and inventory the contents. The notary public shall then file with the lessor a certificate under seal which states the date of the opening of the safe deposit box, the name of the lessee, and a list of the contents. Within 10 days of the opening of the safe deposit box, a copy of this certificate must be mailed to the lessee at his last known postal address.

Civil Practice Law and Rules — Rule 3113[4]

[Conduct of the examination.]

This rule authorizes a deposition to be taken before a notary public in a civil proceeding.

---

[4] Statutory language of this section is summarized and not reprinted verbatim.

Domestic Relations Law — § 11[5]
[By whom a marriage must be solemnized.]

A notary public has no authority to solemnize marriages; nor may a notary public take the acknowledgment of parties and witnesses to a written contract of marriage.

Public Officers Law — § 10[5]
[Official oaths.]

Official oaths, permits the oath of a public officer to be administered by a notary public.

RESTRICTIONS AND VIOLATIONS

Index

Judiciary Law

§ 484. None but attorneys to practice in the state.

No natural person shall ask or receive, directly or indirectly, compensation for appearing for a person other than himself as an attorney in any court or before any magistrate, or for preparing deeds, mortgages, assignments, discharges, leases or any other instrument affecting real estate, wills, codicils, or any other instrument affecting the disposition of property after death, or decedents' estates, or pleadings of any kind in any action brought before any court of record in this state, or make it a business to practice for another as an attorney in any court or before any magistrate unless he has been regularly admitted to practice, as an attorney or

---

[5] Statutory language of this section is summarized and not reprinted verbatim.

counselor, in the courts of record in this state; but nothing in this section shall apply (1) to officers of societies for the prevention of cruelty, duly appointed, when exercising the special powers conferred upon such corporations under section 1403 of the not-for-profit corporation law; or (2) to law students who have completed at least two semesters of law school or persons who have graduated from a law school, who have taken the examination for admittance to practice law in the courts of record in the state immediately available after graduation from law school, or the examination immediately available after being notified by the board of law examiners that they failed to pass said exam, and who have not been notified by the board of law examiners that they have failed to pass two such examinations, acting under the supervision of a legal aid organization, when such students and persons are acting under a program approved by the appellate division of the supreme court of the department in which the principal office of such organization is located and specifying the extent to which such students and persons may engage in activities prohibited by this statute; or (3) to persons who have graduated from a law school approved pursuant to the rules of the court of appeals for the admission of attorneys and counselors-at-law and who have taken the examination for admission to practice as an attorney and counselor-at-law immediately available after graduation from law school or the examination immediately available after being notified by the board of law examiners that they failed to pass said exam, and who have not been notified by the board of law examiners that they have failed to pass two such examinations, when persons are acting under the supervision of the state or a subdivision thereof or of any officer or agency of the state or a subdivision thereof, pursuant to a program approved by the appellate division of the supreme court of the department within which such activities are taking place and specifying the extent to which they may engage in activities otherwise prohibited by this statute and those powers of the supervising governmental entity or officer in connection with which they may engage in such activities.

§ 485. Violation of certain preceding sections a misdemeanor.

Any person violating the provisions of section 478, 479, 480, 481, 482, 483 or 484, shall be guilty of a misdemeanor.

§ 750. Power of courts to punish for criminal contempts.

* * * B.* * * the supreme court has power under this section to punish for a criminal contempt any person who unlawfully practices or assumes to practice law; and a proceeding under this subdivision may be instituted on the court's own motion or on the motion of any officer charged with the duty of investigating or prosecuting unlawful practice of law, or by any bar association incorporated under the laws of this state.

Illegal practice of law by notary public.

To make it a business to practice as an attorney at law, not being a lawyer, is a crime. "Counsel and advice, the drawing of agreements, the organization of corporations and preparing papers connected therewith, the drafting of legal documents of all kinds, including wills, are activities which have been long classed as law practice." (*People v. Alfani*, 227 NY 334, 339.)

Wills.

The execution of wills under the supervision of a notary public acting in effect as a lawyer, "cannot be too strongly condemned, not only for the reason that it means an invasion of the legal profession, but for the fact that testators thereby run the risk of frustrating their own solemnly declared intentions and rendering worthless maturely considered plans for the disposition of estates whose creation may have been the fruit of lives of industry and self-denial." (*Matter of Flynn*, 142 Misc. 7.)

Public Officers Law

Notary must not act before taking and filing oath of office. The Public Officer's Law (§ 15) provides that a person who executes any of the functions of a public office without having taken and duly filed the required oath of office, as prescribed by law, is guilty of a misdemeanor. A notary public is a public officer.

§ 67. Fees of public officers.

1. Each public officer upon whom a duty is expressly imposed by law, must execute the same without fee or reward, except where a fee or other compensation therefor is expressly allowed by law.

2. An officer or other person, to whom a fee or other compensation is allowed by law, for any service, shall not charge or receive a greater fee or reward, for that service, than is so allowed.

3. An officer, or other person, shall not demand or receive any fee or compensation, allowed to him by law for any service, unless the service was actually rendered by him; except that an officer may demand in advance his fee, where he is, by law, expressly directed or permitted to require payment thereof, before rendering the service.

4. * * * An officer or other person, who violates either of the provisions contained in this section, is liable, in addition to the punishment prescribed by law for the criminal offense, to an action in behalf of the person aggrieved, in which the plaintiff is entitled to treble damages.

A notary public subjects himself to criminal prosecution, civil suit and possible removal by asking or receiving more than the statutory allowance, for administering the ordinary oath in connection with an affidavit. (Op. Atty. Gen. (1917) 12 St. Dept. Rep. 507.)

§ 69. Fee for administering certain official oaths prohibited.

An officer is not entitled to a fee, for administering the oath of office to a member of the legislature, to any military officer, to an inspector of election, clerk of the poll, or to any other public office or public employee.

Executive Law
Misconduct by a notary and removal from office.

A notary public who, in the performance of the duties of such office shall practice any fraud or deceit, is guilty of a misdemeanor (Executive Law, § 135-a), and may be removed from office. The notary may be removed from office if the notary made a misstatement of a material fact in his application for appointment; for preparing and taking an oath of an affiant to a statement that the notary knew to be false or fraudulent.

Penal Law
§ 70.00 Sentence of imprisonment for felony.

* * * 2. Maximum term of sentence. The maximum term of an indeterminate sentence shall be at least three years and the term shall be fixed as follows:

* * * (d) For a class D felony, the term shall be fixed by the court, and shall not exceed seven years;

(e) For a class E felony, the term shall be fixed by the court, and shall not exceed four years.* * *

§ 70.15 Sentences of imprisonment for misdemeanors and violation.

1. Class A misdemeanor. A sentence of imprisonment for a class A misdemeanor shall be a definite sentence. When such a sentence is imposed the term shall be fixed by the court, and shall not exceed one year;* * *

§ 170.10 Forgery in the second degree.

A person is guilty of forgery in the second degree when, with intent to defraud, deceive or injure another, he falsely makes, completes or alters a written instrument which is or purports to be, or which is calculated to become or to represent if completed:

1. A deed, will, codicil, contract assignment, commercial instrument, or other instrument which does or may evidence, create, transfer, terminate or otherwise affect a legal right, interest, obligation or status; or

2. A public record, or an instrument filed or required or authorized by law to be filed in or with a public office or public servant; or

3. A written instrument officially issued or created by a public office, public servant or governmental instrumentality.

* * * Forgery in the second degree is a class D felony.

§ 175.40 Issuing a false certificate.

A person is guilty of issuing a false certificate when, being a public servant authorized by law to make or issue official certificates or other official written instruments, and with intent to defraud, deceive or injure another person, he issues such an instrument, or makes the same with intent that it be issued, knowing it contains a false statement or false information.

Issuing a false certificate is a class E felony.

§ 195.00 Official misconduct.

A public servant is guilty of official misconduct when, with intent to obtain a benefit or to injure or deprive another person of a benefit:

1. He commits an act relating to his office but constituting an unauthorized exercise of his official functions, knowing that such act is unauthorized; or

2. He knowingly refrains from performing a duty which is imposed upon him by law or is clearly inherent in the nature of his office.

Official misconduct is a class A misdemeanor.

Notary must officiate on request.

The Penal Law (§ 195.00) provides that an officer before whom an oath of affidavit may be taken is bound to administer the same when requested, and a refusal to do so is a misdemeanor. (*People v. Brooks*, 1 Den. 457.)

Perjury.

One is guilty of perjury if he has stated or given testimony on a material matter, under oath or by affirmation, as to the truth thereof, when he knew the statement or testimony to be false and willfully made.

DEFINITIONS AND GENERAL TERMS

Acknowledgment — A formal declaration before a duly authorized officer by a person who has executed an instrument that such execution is his act and deed.

Technically, an "acknowledgment" is the declaration of a person described in and who has executed a written instrument, that he e:. 'ed the same. As commonly used, the term means the certificate of an officer, duly empowered to take an acknowledgment or proof of the conveyance of real property, that **on a specified date "before me came _____ , to me known to be the individual described in and who executed the foregoing instrument and acknowledged that he executed the same."** The purposes of the law respecting acknowledgments are not only to promote the security of land titles and to prevent frauds in conveyancing, but to furnish proof of the due execution of conveyances (*Armstrong v. Combs*, 15 App. Div. 246) so as to permit the document to be given in evidence, without further proof of its execution, and make it a recordable instrument.

The Real Property Law prescribes:

"§ 303. Requisites of acknowledgments. An acknowledgment must not be taken by any officer unless he knows or has satisfactory evidence, that the person making it is the person described in and who executed such instrument."

The thing to be known is the identity of the person making the acknowledgment with the person described in the instrument and the person who executed the same. This knowledge must be possessed by the notary (*Gross v. Rowley*, 147 App. Div. 529), and a notary must not take an acknowledgment unless the notary knows or has proof that the person making it is the person described in and who executed the instrument (*People v. Kempner,* 49 App. Div. 121). It is not essential that the person who executed the instrument sign his name in the presence of the notary.

Taking acknowledgments over the telephone is illegal and a notary public is guilty of a misdemeanor in so acting. **In the certificate of acknowledgment a notary public declares: "On this _____ day of _____ 19 ___, before me came _____ to me known,"** etc. Unless the person purporting to have made the acknowledgment actually and personally appeared before the notary on the day specified, the notary's certificate that he so came is palpably false and fraudulent. (*Matter of Brooklyn Bar Assoc.,* 225 App. Div. 680.)

Interest as a disqualification. A notary public should not take an acknowledgment to a legal instrument to which the notary is a party in interest. (*Armstrong c. Combs,* 15 App. Div. 246.)

Fraudulent certificates of acknowledgment. A notary public who knowingly makes a false certificate that a deed or other written instrument was acknowledged by a party thereto is guilty of forgery in the second degree, which is punishable by imprisonment for a term of not exceeding seven years (Penal Law, §§ 170.10 and 70.00 [2(d)]. The essence of the crime is false certification, intention to defraud. (*People v. Abeel,* 182 NY 415.) While the absence of guilty knowledge or criminal intent would absolve the notary from criminal liability, the conveyance, of which the false certification is an essential part, is a forgery and, therefore, invalid. (*Caccioppoli v. Lemmo,* 152 App. Div. 650.)

Damages recoverable from notary for false certificate. Action for damages sustained where notary certified that mortgagor had appeared and acknowledged a mortgage. (*Kainz v. Goldsmith,* 231 App. Div. 171.)

Administrator — A person appointed by the court to manage the estate of a deceased person who left no will.

Affiant — The person who makes and subscribes his signature to an affidavit.

Affidavit — An affidavit is a signed statement, duly sworn to, by the maker thereof, before a notary public or other officer authorized to administer oaths. The venue, or county wherein the affidavit was sworn to should be accurately stated. But it is of far more importance that the affiant, the person making the affidavit, should have personally appeared before the notary and have made oath to the statements contained in the affidavit as required by law. Under the Penal Law (§ 210.00) the wilful making of a false affidavit is perjury, but to sustain an indictment therefor, there must have been, in some form, in the presence of an officer authorized to administer an oath, an unequivocal and present act by which the affiant consciously took upon himself the obligation of an oath; his silent delivery of a signed affidavit to the notary for his certificate, is not enough. (*People v. O'Reilly*, 86 NY 154; People ex rel. *Greene v. Swasey*, 122 Misc. 388; *People v. Levitas* (1963) 40 Misc. 2d 331.) A notary public will be removed from office for preparing and taking the oath of an affiant to a statement that the notary knew to be false. (*Matter of Senft*, August 8, 1929; *Matter of Trotta*, February 20, 1930; *Matter of Kibbe*, December 24, 1931.)

The distinction between the taking of an acknowledgment and an affidavit must be clearly understood. In the case of an acknowledgement, the notary public certifies as to the identity and execution of a document; the affidavit involves the administration of an oath to the affiant. There are certain acknowledgment forms which are a combination of an acknowledgment and affidavit. It is incumbent on the notary public to scrutinize each document presented to him and to ascertain the exact nature of the notary's duty with relation thereto.

An affidavit differs from a deposition in that an affidavit is an ex parte statement. (*See definition of Deposition.*)

Affirmation — A solemn declaration made by persons who conscientiously decline taking an oath; it is equivalent to an oath and is just as binding; if a person has religious or conscientious scruples against taking an oath, the notary public should have the person affirm. **The following is a form of affirmation:**

"Do you solemnly, sincerely, and truly, declare and affirm that the statements made by you are true and correct."

Apostille — Department of State authentication attached to a notarized and county-certified document for possible international use.

Attest — To witness the execution of a written instrument, at the request of the person who makes it, and subscribe the same as a witness.

Attestation Clause — That clause (e.g. at the end of a will) wherein the witnesses certify that the instrument has been executed before them, and the manner of the execution of the same.

Authentication (Notarial) — A certificate subjoined by a county clerk to any certificate of proof or acknowledgment or oath signed by a notary; this county clerk's certificate authenticates or verifies the authority of the notary public to act as such. (See section 133, Executive Law.)

Bill of Sale — A written instrument given to pass title of personal property from vendor to vendee.

Certified Copy — A copy of a public record signed and certified as a true copy by the public official having custody of the original. A notary public has no authority to issue certified copies. Notaries must not certify to the authenticity of legal documents and other papers required to be filed with foreign consular officers. Within this prohibition are certificates of the following type:

United States of America)
State of New York   ) ss.
County of New York   )

"I _____, a notary public of the State of New York, in and for the county of _____, duly commissioned, qualified and sworn according to the laws of the State of New York, do hereby certify and declare that I verily believe the annexed instrument executed by _____ and sworn to before _____, a notary public of the State of _____, to be true and genuine in every respect, and that full faith and credit are and ought to be given thereto. "In testimony whereof I have hereunto set my hand and seal at the City of _____, this _____ day of _____, 19__.

(Seal)   (Notarial Signature.)"

Concerning such a notarial certificate it has been held:

"The law has made specific provisions for the manner in which papers may be certified as to authenticity and originality. While in this individual case there may be no indication of deceiving nor any deception, nevertheless it is a practice which may become subject to deception and therefore the requirements as laid down by the law for the conduct of notaries should be most strictly enforced." (Op. Atty. Gen.)

The making of a useless certificate and the collection of a fee therefore, by a notary public, after the notary has had official warning against such practices, justifies a conclusion of misconduct which warrants the notary's removal from office. (Op. Atty. Gen., May 26, 1931.) But a notarial certificate that an attached copy of a paper is a true and exact copy of the original document is not within the ban of the last mentioned opinion, for the reason that while this form of certificate does not permit the copy of the paper to be read in evidence, it might be accepted by certain persons as sufficient proof of the correctness of the copy and, accordingly, it cannot be said to be entirely valueless. (Op. Atty. Gen., Aug. 22, 1933.)

Chattel — Personal property, such as household goods or fixtures.

Chattel Paper — A writing or writings which evidence both an obligation to pay money and a security interest in a lease or specific goods. The agreement which creates or provides for the security interest is known as a security agreement.

Codicil — An instrument made subsequent to a will and modifying it in some respects.

Consideration — Anything of value given to induce entering into a contract; it may be money, personal services, or even love and affection.

Contempt of Court — Behavior disrespectful of the authority of a court which disrupts the execution of court orders.

Contract — An agreement between competent parties to do or not to do certain things for a legal consideration, whereby each party acquires a right to what the other possesses.

Conveyance (Deed) — Every instrument, in writing, except a will, by which any estate or interest in real property is created, transferred, assigned or surrendered.

County Clerk's Certificate — See "Authentication (Notarial)."

Deponent — One who makes oath to a written statement. Technically, a person subscribing a deposition but used interchangeably with "Affiant."

Deposition — The testimony of a witness taken out of court or other hearing proceeding, under oath or by affirmation, before a notary public or other person, officer or commissioner before whom such testimony is authorized by law to be taken, which is intended to be used at the trial or hearing.

Duress — Unlawful constraint exercised upon a person whereby he is forced to do some act against his will.

Escrow — The placing of an instrument in the hands of a person as a depository who on the happening of a designated event, is to deliver the instrument to a third person. This agreement, once established, should be unalterable.

Executor — One named in a will to carry out the provisions of the will.

Ex Parte (from one side only) — A hearing or examination in the presence of, or on papers filed by, one party and in the absence of the other.

Felony — A crime punishable by death or imprisonment in a state prison.

Guardian — A person in charge of a minor's person or property.

Judgment — Decree of a court declaring that one individual is indebted to another and fixing the amount of such indebtedness.

Jurat — A jurat is that part of an affidavit where the officer (notary public) certifies that it was sworn to before him. It is not the affidavit.

The following is the form of jurat generally employed:

"Sworn to before me this _____ day of _____, 19___."

Those words placed directly after the signature on the affidavit stating that the facts therein contained were sworn to or affirmed before the officer (notary public) together with his official signature and such other data as required by section 137 of the Executive Law.

Laches — The delay or negligence in asserting one's legal rights.

Lease — A contract whereby, for a consideration, usually termed rent, one who is entitled to the possession of real property transfers such right to another for life, for a term of years or at will.

Lien — A legal right or claim upon a specific property which attaches to the property until a debt is satisfied.

Litigation — The act of carrying on a lawsuit.

Misdemeanor — Any crime other than a felony.

Mortgage on Real Property — An instrument in writing, duly executed and delivered that creates a lien upon real estate as security for the payment of a specified debt, which is usually in the form of a bond.

Notary Public — A public officer who executes acknowledgments of deeds or writings in order to render them available as evidence of the facts therein contained; administers oaths and affirmations as to the truth of statements contained in papers or documents requiring the administration of an oath. The notary's general authority is defined in section 135 of the Executive Law; the notary has certain other powers which can be found in the various provisions of law set forth earlier in this publication.

Oath — A verbal pledge given by the person taking it that his statements are made under an immediate sense of his responsibility to God, who will punish the affiant if the statements are false.

Notaries public must administer oaths and affirmations in manner and form as prescribed by the Civil Practice Law and Rules, namely:

§ 2309(b) Form. An oath or affirmation shall be administered in a form calculated to awaken the conscience and impress the mind of the person taking it in accordance with his religious or ethical beliefs.

An oath must be administered as required by law. The person taking the oath must personally appear before the notary; an oath cannot be administered over the telephone (*Matter of Napolis*, 169 App. Div. 469), and the oath must be administered in the form required by the statute (*Bookman v. City of New York*, 200 NY 53, 56).

When an oath is administered the person taking the oath must express assent to the oath repeated by the notary by the words "I do" or some other words of like meaning.

For an oath or affirmation to be valid, whatever form is adopted, it is necessary that: first, the person swearing or affirming must personally be in the presence of the notary public; secondly, that the person unequivocally swears or affirms that what he states is true; thirdly, that he swears or affirms as of that time; and, lastly, that the person conscientiously takes upon himself the obligation of an oath.

A notary public does not fulfill his duty by merely asking a person whether the signature on a purported affidavit is his. An oath must be administered.

A corporation or partnership cannot take an oath; an oath must be taken by an individual.

A notary public cannot administer an oath to himself.

The privileges and rights of a notary public are personal and cannot be delegated to anyone.

Plaintiff — A person who starts a suit or brings an action against another.

Power of Attorney — A written statement by an individual giving another person the power to act for him.

Proof — The formal declaration made by a subscribing witness to the execution of an instrument setting forth his place of residence, that he knew the person described in and who executed the instrument and that he saw such person execute such instrument.

Protest — A formal statement in writing by a notary public, under seal, that a certain bill of exchange or promissory note was on a certain day presented for payment, or acceptance, and that such payment or acceptance was refused.

Seal — The laws of the State of New York do not require the use of seals by notaries public. If a seal is used, it should sufficiently identify the notary public, his authority and jurisdiction. It is the opinion of the Department of State that the only inscription required is the name of the notary and the words "Notary Public for the State of New York."

Signature of Notary Public — A notary public must sign the name under which he was appointed and no other. In addition to his signature and venue, the notary public shall print, typewrite or stamp beneath his signature in black ink, his name, the words "Notary Public State of New York," the name of the county in which he is qualified, and the date upon which his commission expires (section 137, Executive Law).

When a woman notary marries during the term of office for which she was appointed, she may continue to use her maiden name as notary public. However, if she elects to use her marriage name, then for the balance of her term as a notary public she must continue to use her maiden name in her signature and seal when acting in her notarial capacity, adding after her signature her married name, in parentheses. When renewing her commission as a notary public, she may apply under her married name or her maiden name. She must then perform all her notarial functions under the name selected.

A member of a religious order, known therein by a name other than his secular cognomen, may be appointed and may officiate as a notary public under the name by which he is known in religious circles. (Op. Atty. Gen., Mar. 20, 1930.)

Statute — A law established by an act of the Legislature.

Statute of Frauds — State law which provides that certain contracts must be in writing or partially complied with, in order to be enforceable at law.

Statute of Limitations — A law that limits the time within which a criminal prosecution or civil action must be started.

Subordination Clause — A clause which permits the placing of a mortgage at a later date which takes priority over an existing mortgage.

Sunday — A notary public may administer an oath or take an affidavit or acknowledgment on Sunday. However, a deposition cannot be taken on Sunday in a civil proceeding.

Swear — This term includes every mode authorized by law for administering an oath.

Taking an Acknowledgment — The act of the person named in an instrument telling the notary public that he is the person named in the instrument and acknowledging that he executed such instrument; also includes the act of the notary public in obtaining satisfactory evidence of the identity of the person whose acknowledgment is taken.

The notary public "certifies to the taking of the acknowledgment" when the notary signs his official signature to the form setting forth the fact of the taking of the acknowledgment.

Venue — The geographical place where a notary public takes an affidavit or acknowledgment. Every affidavit or certificate of acknowledgment should show on its face the venue of the notarial act. The venue is usually set forth at the beginning of the instrument or at the top of the notary's jurat, or official certification, as follows: "State of New York, County of (New York) ss.:". Section 137 of the Executive Law imposes the duty on the notary public to include the venue of his act in all certificates of acknowledgments or jurats to affidavits.

Will — The disposition of one's property to take effect after death.

SCHEDULE OF FEES

Appointment as Notary Public	$20.00
Change of Name/Address	10.00
Duplicate Identification Card	10.00
Filing Signature and Oath of Office	10.00
Issuance of Certificate of Official Character	5.00
Filing Certificate of Official Character	10.00
Authentication Certificate	3.00
Protest of Note, Commercial Paper, etc.	.75
Each additional Notice of Protest (limit 5) each	.10
Oath or Affirmation	2.00
Acknowledgment (each person)	2.00
Proof of Execution (each person)	2.00
Swearing Witness	2.00

NOTE: *Where gender pronouns appear in this booklet, they are meant to refer to both male and female persons.*

ADDITIONAL STATUTES
PERTAINING TO NEW YORK NOTARIES

Real Property Law

§ 300. Acknowledgments and proofs by persons in or with the armed forces of the United States.

The acknowledgment or proof of a conveyance of real property situate in this state, if made by a person enlisted or commissioned in or serving in or with the armed forces of the United States or by a dependent of any such person, wherever located, or by a person attached to or accompanying the armed forces of the United States, whether made within or without the United States, may be made before any commissioned officer in active service of the armed forces of the United States with the rank of second lieutenant or higher in the Army, Air Force or Marine Corps, or ensign or higher in the Navy or

Coast Guard, or with the equivalent rank in any other component part of the armed forces of the United States.

In addition to the requirements of sections three hundred three, three hundred four, and three hundred six of this chapter, the certificate of acknowledgment or proof taken under this section shall state (a) the rank and serial number of the officer taking the same, and the command to which he is attached, (b) that the person making such acknowledgment or proof was, at the time of making the same, enlisted or commissioned in or serving in or with the armed forces of the United States or the dependent of such a person, or a person attached to or accompanying the armed forces of the United States, and (c) the serial number of the person who makes, or whose dependent makes the acknowledgment or proof if such person is enlisted or commissioned in the armed forces of the United States. The place where such acknowledgment or proof is taken need not be disclosed.

No authentication of the officer's certificate of acknowledgment or proof shall be required.

Notwithstanding any of the provisions of this section, the acknowledgment or proof of a conveyance of real property situate in this state may also be made as provided in sections two hundred ninety-eight, two hundred ninety-nine, two hundred ninety-nine-a, three hundred one, and three hundred one-a, of this chapter.[6]

§ 309-a. Uniform forms of certificate of acknowledgment or proof.

1. The certificate of an acknowledgment, within this state, of a conveyance or other instrument in respect to real property situate in this state, by a person, may[7] conform substantially with the following form, the blanks being properly filled:

```
State of New York        )
                         )  ss.:
County of _____    )
```

On the _____ day of _____ in the year _____ before me, the undersigned, a Notary Public in and for said State, personally appeared _____, personally known to me or proved to me on the basis of satisfactory evidence to be the individual(s) whose name(s) is (are) subscribed to the within instrument and acknowledged to me that he/she/they executed the same in his/her/their authorized capacity(ies), and that by his/her/their signature(s) on the instrument, the individual(s), or the person upon behalf of which the individual(s) acted, executed the instrument.

(Signature and office of individual taking acknowledgment.)

---

[6] Section 298 and Section 300 are included in this *Primer*. Sections 299, 299-a and 300-a, relating to acknowledgments and proofs taken by armed forces personnel or in places outside of the United States, are not included

[7] Effective September 1, 1999, the word "may" becomes "must."

2. The certificate for a proof of execution by subscribing witness, within this state, of a conveyance or other instrument made by any person in respect to real property situate in this state, may[8] conform substantially with the following form, the blanks being properly filled:

> State of New York   )
>   ) ss.:
> County of _____)
>   On the _____ day of _____ in the year _____ before me, the undersigned, a Notary Public in and for said State, personally appeared _____, the subscribing witness to the foregoing instrument, with whom I am personally acquainted, who, being by me duly sworn, did depose and say that he/she/they reside(s) in _____ (if the place of residence is in a city, include the street and street number, if any, thereof); that he/she/they know(s) _____ to be the individual described in and who executed the foregoing instrument; that said subscribing witness was present and saw said _____ execute the same; and that said witness at the same time subscribed his/her/their name(s) as a witness thereto.

(Signature and office of individual taking proof.)

3. A certificate of an acknowledgment or proof taken under section three hundred of this article shall include additional information required by that section.

4. For the purposes of this section, the term "person" means any corporation, joint stock company, estate, general partnership (including any registered limited liability partnership or foreign limited liability partnership), limited liability company (including a professional service limited liability company), foreign limited liability company (including a foreign professional service limited liability company), joint venture, limited partnership, natural person, attorney in fact, real estate investment trust, business trust or other trust, custodian, nominee or any other individual or entity in its own or any representative capacity.

[9]5. No provision of this section shall be construed to prohibit the use of any other or different form of certificate of acknowledgment or certificate for proof by a subscribing witness which meets the requirements of this article exclusive of this section. ■

---

[8] Effective September 1, 1999, the word "may" becomes "must."
[9] Effective September 1, 1999, this subdivision 5 is repealed.

Offices of the New York Department of State

The following offices of the New York Department of State may provide applications for Notary Public appointments. All first-time applications must be mailed to the Albany office. Applications for renewal are processed through the local County Clerk's office.

Albany
New York Department of State
Division of Licensing Services
84 Holland Avenue
Albany, NY 12208-3490
Tel: 1-518-474-4429
Fax: 1-518-473-6648

Binghamton
State Office Building Annex
44 Hawley St., 15th Floor
Binghamton, NY 13901
1-607-721-8757

Buffalo
State Office Building
65 Court St.
Buffalo, NY 14202
1-716-847-7110

Hauppuage
Suffolk State Office Building
Veterans Memorial Highway
Hauppuage, NY 11788
1-516-952-6579

New York City
State Office Building
270 Broadway
New York, NY 10007
1-212-417-5747

Syracuse
Hughes State Office
Building
333 E. Washington St.,
Room 514
Syracuse, NY 13202
1-315-428-4258

Utica
State Office Building
207 Genesee St.
Utica, NY 13501
1-315-793-2533

County Clerks' Offices

Within two years of taking the Notary exam, the first-time Notary must file the exam slip, application and oath of office with the Department of State (see page 104). However, Notaries seeking renewal should file the oath and application with their local County Clerk's office.

At these same offices, certificates authenticating a local Notary's signature and seal may be obtained by anyone presenting a document notarized by a particular local Notary.

For certified copies of marriage certificates, contact the office of the County Clerk where the certificate was filed.

Albany County
County Court House
Rm. 128
Albany, NY 12207
1-518-487-5000

Allegany County
County Office Bldg.
7 Court St.
Belmont, NY 14813
1-716-268-9270

Bronx County
851 Grand Concourse,
Rm. 118
Bronx, NY 10451
1-212-590-3644

Broome County
44 Hawley St.
Binghamton, NY 13902
1-607-772-2451

Cattaraugus County
Cattaraugus County
Center
303 Court St.
Little Valley, NY 14755
1-716-938-9111

Cayuga County
Cayuga County Office
Bldg.
160 Genesee St., 1st Fl.
Auburn, NY 13021
1-315-253-1271

Chautauqua County
P.O. Box 170
Mayville, NY 14757
1-716-753-7111

Chemung County
210 Lake St.
Elmira, NY 14901
1-607-737-2920

Chenango County
County Office Bldg.
Norwich, NY 13815
1-607-335-4573

Clinton County
137 Margaret St.
Plattsburgh, NY 12901
1-518-565-4700

Columbia County
Court House
405 Union St.
Hudson, NY 12534
1-518-828-3339

Cortland County
Court House
P.O. Box 5590
Cortland, NY 13045
1-607-753-5021

Delaware County
P.O Box 426
Delhi, NY 13753
1-607-746-2123

Dutchess County
County Office Bldg.
22 Market St.
Poughkeepsie,
NY 12601
1-914-431-1856

Erie County
25 Delaware Ave.
Buffalo, NY 14202
1-716-858-8785

Essex County
100 Court St.
P.O. Box 247
Elizabethtown,
NY 12932
1-518-873-3600

Franklin County
Court House
63 W. Main St.
Malone, NY 12953
1-518-483-6767, Ex. 203

Fulton County
P.O. Box 485
Johnstown, NY 12095
1-518-762-0555

Genesee County
P.O. Box 379
Batavia, NY 14021
1-716-344-2550

Greene County
P.O. Box 446
Catskill, NY 12414
1-518-943-2050

Hamilton County
Route 8, P.O. Box 204
Lake Pleasant,
NY 12180
1-518-548-7111

Herkimer County
County Office Bldg.
P.O. Box 111
Herkimer, NY 13350
1-315-867-1002

Jefferson County
County Clerk Bldg.
175 Arsenal St.
Watertown, NY 13601
1-315-785-3081

Kings County
Supreme Court Bldg.
360 Adams St.,
Rm. 188
Brooklyn, NY 11201
1-718-643-8011

Lewis County
7660 State St.
Lowville, NY 13367
1-315-376-2414

Livingston County
County Govt. Center
6 Court St., Rm. 201
Geneseo, NY 14454
1-716-243-7000

Madison County
County Office Bldg.
Wampsville, NY 13163
1-315-366-2261

Monroe County
County Bldg.
39 W. Main St.,
Rm. 101
Rochester, NY 14614
1-716-428-5151

Montgomery County
County Office Bldg.
P.O. Box 1500
Fonda, NY 12068
1-518-853-3431

Nassau County
240 Old Country Rd.
Mineola, NY 11501
1-516-571-2861,
1-516-571-1445

New York County
60 Centre St.
New York, NY 10007
1-212-374-8589,
1-212-374-8587

Niagara County
175 Hawley St.
P.O. Box 461
Lockport, NY
14094-0461
1-716-439-7022

Oneida County
County Office Bldg.
800 Park Ave.
Utica, NY 13501
1-315-798-5773

Onondaga County
401 Montgomery St.,
Rm. 200
Syracuse, NY 13202
1-315-435-2226,
1-315-435-2241

Ontario County
25 Pleasant St.
Canandaigua,
NY 14424
1-716-396-4200

Orange County
Orange County Govt.
Center
255 Main St.
Goshen, NY 10924
1-914-294-5151, Ex. 1219

Orleans County
Main St.
Albion, NY 14411
1-716-589-5334

Oswego County
County Office Bldg.
46 East Bridge
Oswego, NY 13126
1-315-349-8385

Otsego County
County Office Bldg.
197 Main St.
Cooperstown,
NY 13326
1-607-547-4200

Putnam County
2 County Center
Carmel, NY 10512
1-914-225-3641, Ex. 300

Queens County
General Court House
88-11 Sutphin Blvd.
Jamaica, NY 11435
1-718-520-3702

Rensselaer County
Court House
Congress & 2nd Sts.
Troy, NY 12180
1-518-270-4080

Richmond County
Court House
18 Richmond Terrace
Staten Island,
NY 10301
1-718-390-5386

Rockland County
27 New Hempstead
Rd.
New City, NY 10956
1-914-638-5069

St. Lawrence County
48 Court St.
Canton, NY 13617
1-315-379-2237

Saratoga County
County Office Bldg.
40 McMaster St.
Ballston Spa, NY 12020
1-518-885-2213

Schenectady County
County Office Bldg.
620 State St.
Schenectady,
NY 12305
1-518-388-4220

Schoharie County
P.O. Box 549
Schoharie, NY 12157
1-518-295-8316

Schuyler County
105 Ninth St.
Watkins Glen,
NY 14891
1-607-535-2132

Seneca County
1 DiPronio Dr.
Waterloo, NY 13165
1-315-539-5655

Steuben County
3 Pulteney Square
Bath, NY 14810
1-607-776-9631

Suffolk County
310 Center Dr.
Riverhead, NY 11901
1-516-852-2000

Sullivan County
County Office Bldg.
Monticello, NY 12701
1-914-794-3000, Ex. 3160

Tioga County
16 Court St.
Owego, NY 13827
1-607-687-3133

Tompkins County
Court House
320 N. Tioga St.
Ithaca, NY 14850
1-607-274-5431

Ulster County
244 Fair St.
P.O. Box 1800
Kingston, NY 12401
1-914-331-9300, Ex. 265

Warren County
Municipal Center
Lake George,
NY 12845
1-518-761-6429

Washington County
Upper Broadway
Fort Edward, NY 12828
1-518-747-3374

Wayne County
9 Pearl St.
P.O. Box 608
Lyons, NY 14489
1-315-946-5972

Westchester County
110 Grove St., Rm. 330
White Plains,
NY 10601
1-914-285-3070

Wyoming County
143 N. Main St.
P.O. Box 70
Warsaw, NY 14569
1-716-786-8810

Yates County
110 Court St.
Penn Yan, NY 14527
1-315-536-5120

Bureaus of Vital Statistics

New York Notaries are not authorized by law to certify copies. Persons requesting "notarization," "certification" or certified copies of birth or death certificates should be referred to the appropriate public Bureau of Vital Statistics. The following state agencies can provide certified copies of birth and death records for persons who were born or have died in the respective states, as can certain local offices not listed here.

Alabama
Center for Health Statistics
State Dept. of Public Health
P.O. Box 5625
Montgomery, AL 36103-5625
1-205-242-5033

Alaska
Dept. of Health & Social Services
Bureau of Vital Statistics
P.O. Box H-02G
Juneau, AK 99811-0675
1-907-465-3391

Arizona
Vital Records Section
Arizona Dept. of Health Services
P.O. Box 3887
Phoenix, AZ 85030
1-602-255-3260

Arkansas
Div. of Vital Records, Dept. of Health
4815 West Markham St.
Little Rock, AR 72201
1-501-661-2336

California
Vital Statistics Section
Dept. of Health Services
P.O. Box 730241
Sacramento, CA 94244-0241
1-916-445-2684

Colorado
Vital Records Section, Dept. of Health
4300 Cherry Creek Drive South
Denver, CO 80222-1530
1-303-756-4464

Connecticut
Vital Records, Dept. of Health Services
150 Washington St.
Hartford, CT 06106
1-203-566-2334

Delaware
Office of Vital Statistics
Div. of Public Health
P.O. Box 637
Dover, DE 19903
1-302-739-4721

District of Columbia
Vital Records Branch
425 I St., N.W., Rm. 3009
Washington, DC 20001
1-202-727-9281

Florida
Dept. of Health & Rehabilitative Svs.
Office of Vital Statistics
1217 Pearl St.
P.O. Box 210
Jacksonville, FL 32231
1-850-359-6900

Georgia
Georgia Dept. of Human Resources
Vital Records Unit
47 Trinity Avenue, S.W., Rm. 217-H
Atlanta, GA 30334
1-404-656-4900

Hawaii
Office of Health Status Monitoring
State Dept. of Health
P.O. Box 3378
Honolulu, HI 96801
1-808-586-4533

Idaho
Vital Statistics Unit
Idaho Dept. of Health & Welfare
450 West State St.
Statehouse Mail
Boise, ID 83720-9990
1-208-334-5988

Illinois
Div. of Vital Records
Illinois Dept. of Public Health
605 West Jefferson St.
Springfield, IL 62702-5097
1-217-782-6553

Indiana
Vital Records Section
State Dept. of Health
1330 West Michigan St.
P.O. Box 1964
Indianapolis, IN 46206-1964
1-317-633-0274

Iowa
Iowa Dept. of Public Health
Vital Records Section, Lucas Ofc. Bldg.
321 East 12th St.
Des Moines, IA 50319-0075
1-515-281-4944

Kansas
Office of Vital Statistics
Kansas State Dept. of Health &
Environment
900 Jackson St.
Topeka, KS 66612-1290
1-913-296-1400

Kentucky
Office of Vital Statistics
Dept. for Health Services
275 East Main St.
Frankfort, KY 40621
1-502-564-4212

Louisiana
Vital Records Registry
Office of Public Health
325 Loyola Avenue
New Orleans, LA 70112
1-504-568-5152

Maine
Office of Vital Statistics
Maine Dept. of Human Services
State House Station 11
Augusta, ME 04333-0011
1-207-289-3184

Maryland
Div. of Vital Records
Dept. of Health & Mental Hygiene
Metro Executive Bldg.
4201 Patterson Ave.
P.O. Box 68760
Baltimore, MD 21215-0020
1-301-225-5988

Massachusetts
Registry of Vital Records & Statistics
150 Tremont St., Rm. B-3
Boston, MA 02111
1-617-727-7388

Michigan
Office of the State Registrar & Center
for Health Statistics
Michigan Dept. of Public Health
3423 North Logan St.
Lansing, MI 48909
1-517-335-8655

Minnesota
Minnesota Dept. of Health
Section of Vital Statistics
717 Delaware St., S.E.
P.O. Box 9441
Minneapolis, MN 55440
1-612-623-5121

Mississippi
Vital Records, State Dept. of Health
2423 North State St.
Jackson, MS 39216
1-601-960-7450

Missouri
Missouri Dept. of Health
Bureau of Vital Records
1730 East Elm
P.O. Box 570
Jefferson City, MO 65102-0570
1-314-751-6400

Montana
Bureau of Records & Statistics
State Dept. of Health & Environmental
Services
Helena, MT 59620
1-406-444-2614

Nebraska
Bureau of Vital Statistics
State Dept. of Health
301 Centennial Mall South
P.O. Box 95007
Lincoln, NE 68509-5007
1-402-471-2871

Nevada
Div. of Health – Vital Statistics
Capitol Complex
505 East King St., #102
Carson City, NV 89710
1-702-687-4480

New Hampshire
Bureau of Vital Records
Health and Welfare Bldg.
6 Hazen Drive
Concord, NH 03301
1-603-271-4654

New Jersey
State Dept. of Health
Bureau of Vital Statistics
South Warren and Market, CN 370
Trenton, NJ 08625
1-609-292-4087

New Mexico
Vital Statistics
New Mexico Health Services Div.
P.O. Box 26110
Santa Fe, NM 87502
1-505-827-2338

New York State
Vital Records Section
State Dept. of Health
Empire State Plaza, Tower Bldg.
Albany, NY 12237-0023
1-518-474-3075

New York City
Div. of Vital Records
New York City Dept. of Health
P.O. Box 3776
New York, NY 10007
1-212-693-4637

North Carolina
Dept. of Environment, Health &
Natural Resources
Div. of Epidemiology
Vital Records Section
225 North McDowell St., P.O. Box 29537
Raleigh, NC 27626-0537
1-919-733-3526

North Dakota
Div. of Vital Records
State Capitol
600 East Boulevard Avenue
Bismarck, ND 58505
1-701-224-2360

Ohio
Bureau of Vital Statistics
Ohio Dept. of Health
P.O. Box 15098
Columbus, OH 43215-0098
1-614-466-2531

Oklahoma
Oklahoma Vital Records Section
State Dept. of Health
1000 N.E. 10th St., P.O. Box 53551
Oklahoma City, OK 73152
1-405-271-4040

Oregon
Oregon Health Div.
Vital Statistics Section
P.O. Box 14050
Portland, OR 97214-0050
1-503-731-4095

Pennsylvania
Div. of Vital Records
State Dept. of Health, Central Bldg.
101 S. Mercer St., P.O. Box 1528
New Castle, PA 16103
1-412-656-3100

Rhode Island
Div. of Vital Records
Rhode Island Dept. of Health
Rm. 101, Cannon Bldg.
3 Capitol Hill
Providence, RI 02908-5097
1-401-277-2811

South Carolina
Office of Vital Records & Public
Health Statistics
South Carolina Dept. of Health &
Environmental Control
2600 Bull St.
Columbia, SC 29201
1-803-734-4830

South Dakota
State Dept. of Health
Center for Health Policy & Statistics
Vital Records
523 East Capitol
Pierre, SD 57501
1-605-773-3355

Tennessee
Tennessee Vital Records
Dept. of Health, Cordell Hull Bldg.
Nashville, TN 37247-0350
1-615-741-1763

Texas
Bureau of Vital Statistics
Texas Dept. of Health
1100 West 49th St.
Austin, TX 78756-3191
1-512-458-7111

Utah
Bureau of Vital Records
Utah Dept. of Health
288 North 1460 West
P.O. Box 16700
Salt Lake City, UT 84116-0700
1-801-538-6105

Vermont
Vermont Dept. of Health
Vital Records Section
60 Main St., Box 70
Burlington, VT 05402
1-802-828-3286

Virginia
Div. of Vital Records
State Health Dept.
P.O. Box 1000
Richmond, VA 23208-1000
1-804-786-6228

Washington
Dept. of Health
Center for Health Statistics
P.O. Box 9709
Olympia, WA 98507-9709
1-206-753-5936

West Virginia
Vital Registration Office
Div. of Health
State Capitol Complex, Bldg. 3
Charleston, WV 25305
1-304-558-2931

Wisconsin
Vital Records
1 West Wilson St.
P.O. Box 309
Madison, WI 53701
1-608-266-1371

Wyoming
Vital Records Services
Hathaway Bldg.
Cheyenne, WY 82002
1-307-777-7591

American Samoa
Registrar of Vital Statistics
Vital Statistics Section
Government of American Samoa
Pago Pago, AS 96799
1-684-633-1222, ext. 214

Guam
Office of Vital Statistics
Dept. of Public Health & Social
Services
Government of Guam
P.O. Box 2816
Agana, GU, M.I. 96910
1-671-734-4589

Northern Mariana Islands
Superior Court
Vital Records Section
P.O. Box 307
Saipan, MP 96950
1-670-234-6401, ext. 15

Panama Canal Zone
Panama Canal Commission
Vital Statistics Clerk
APOAA 34011

Puerto Rico
Dept. of Health
Demographic Registry
P.O. Box 11854
Fernández Juncos Station
San Juan, PR 00910
1-809-728-7980

Virgin Islands (St. Croix)
Registrar of Vital Statistics
Charles Harwood Memorial Hospital
Christiansted, St. Croix, VI 00820
1-809-774-9000, ext. 4621

**Virgin Islands (St. Thomas,
St. John)**
Registrar of Vital Statistics
Knud Hansen Complex
Hospital Ground
Charlotte Amalie
St. Thomas, VI 00802
1-809-774-9000, ext. 4621

Hague Convention Nations

The nations listed on the following pages are parties to a treaty called the Hague Convention Abolishing the Requirement of Legalization (Authentication) for Foreign Public Documents.

Treaty Simplifies Authentication. A Notary's signature on documents that are sent to these nations may be authenticated (verified as valid for the benefit of the recipient in the foreign nation) by the state that commissioned the Notary through attachment of a single certificate of capacity called an *apostille*. The *apostille* (French for "notation") is the only authentication certificate necessary. Nations not subscribing to the Hague Convention may require as many as five or six separate authenticating certificates from different governmental agencies, domestic and foreign.

Unfortunately, New York also requires the notarized document to bear an authenticating certificate from the County Clerk before issuing an *apostille*.

How to Request an *Apostille*. To obtain an *apostille*, anyone may mail the notarized document, the county clerk's authenticating certificate and a $10 fee per notarized document, payable to the "New York State Department of State," to either:

Department of State	Department of State
Miscellaneous Records	Certification Unit
41 State Street	270 Broadway, 6th Floor
Albany, NY 12231	New York, NY 10007
1-518-474-4770	1-212-417-5687

An *apostille* must be specifically requested, indicating the nation to which the document will be sent.

Hague Convention Nations. The following nations currently participate in the Hague Convention:

Andorra	El Salvador
Angola[1]	Fiji
Antigua and Barbuda	Finland
Argentina[2]	France[5]
Armenia[3]	Germany
Australia	Greece
Austria	Grenada[1]
Bahamas	Guyana
Barbados	Hong Kong[6]
Belarus[3]	Hungary
Belgium	Israel
Belize	Italy
Bosnia-Herzegovina[4]	Japan
Botswana	Kiribati[1]
Brunei	Latvia
Comoros Islands[1]	Lesotho
Croatia[4]	Liberia[7]
Cyprus	Liechtenstein
Djibouti[1]	Luxembourg
Dominica[1]	Macedonia[4]

1. Recently independent country; has not confirmed that the Convention still applies. In accordance with Article 34(l) of the Vienna Convention on Succession of States in Respect of Treaties, the United States' view is that when a country is a party to a multilateral treaty or convention, and that country dissolves, the successor states inherit the treaty obligations of the former government.

2. Excludes recognition of extension of the Convention by the United Kingdom to the Malvinas, South Georgia, South Sandwich Islands and the Argentine Antarctic Sector.

3. Now known as the Newly Independent States. Former Union of Soviet Socialist Republics (U.S.S.R.) had signed on to the Convention, but dissolved prior to its taking effect. Only Armenia, the Belarus Republic and the Russian Federation of the former U.S.S.R. have confirmed that the Convention applies in their jurisdictions.

4. Former Yugoslavia, with its capital in the present Serbia-Montenegro, was a party to the Convention. However, only the breakaway nations of Bosnia-Herzegovina, Croatia, Macedonia and Slovenia have confirmed that the Convention still applies.

5. Including French Overseas Departments of French Guiana, French Polynesia, Guadeloupe, Martinique, New Caledonia, Reunion, St. Pierre and Miquelon, and Wallis and Futuna.

6. Retained status as Hague nation after control of Hong Kong was returned to China on July 1, 1997.

7. Convention does *not* apply between Liberia and the United States.

Malawi	San Marino, Republic of
Malta	Seychelles
Marshall Islands	Slovenia[4]
Mauritius	Solomon Islands[1]
Mexico	South Africa
Mozambique[1]	Spain
Netherlands[8]	Suriname
Norway	Swaziland
Panama	Switzerland
Portugal[9]	Turkey
Russia[3]	Tuvalu[1]
Saint Kitts and Nevis	United Kingdom[10]
Saint Lucia	United States
Saint Vincent and	of America
the Grenadines	Vanuatu[1]

Inquiries. Persons having questions about the Hague Convention Abolishing the Requirement of Legalization for Foreign Public Documents may address their inquiries to:

Office of American Citizens Services
Department of State
Washington, DC 20520
1-202-647-5225

---

1. Recently independent country; has not confirmed that the Convention still applies. In accordance with Article 34(l) of the Vienna Convention on Succession of States in Respect of Treaties, the United States' view is that when a country is a party to a multilateral treaty or convention, and that country dissolves, the successor states inherit the treaty obligations of the former government.

3. Now known as the Newly Independent States. Former Union of Soviet Socialist Republics (U.S.S.R.) had signed on to the Convention, but dissolved prior to its taking effect. Only Armenia, the Belarus Republic and the Russian Federation of the former U.S.S.R. have confirmed that the Convention applies in their jurisdictions.

4. Former Yugoslavia, with its capital in the present Serbia-Montenegro, was a party to the Convention. However, only the breakaway nations of Bosnia-Herzegovina, Croatia, Macedonia and Slovenia have confirmed that the Convention still applies.

8. Extended to Aruba, Curacao and Netherlands Antilles.

9. Extended to Macao and all overseas territories.

10. United Kingdom of Great Britain and Northern Ireland is extended to Anguilla, Bermuda, British Antarctica Territory, British Virgin Islands, Cayman Islands, Falkland Islands, Gibraltar, Guernsey, Isle of Man, Jersey, Montserrat, Saint Georgia and the South Sandwich Islands, Saint Helena, Tonga, Turks and Caicos Islands, and Zimbabwe.

About
the Publisher

Since 1957, The National Notary Association — a nonprofit educational organization — has served the nation's nearly four and a half million Notaries Public with a wide variety of instructional programs and services.

As the country's clearinghouse for information on notarial laws, customs and practices, the NNA educates Notaries through publications, seminars, annual conferences and a Notary Information Service that offers immediate answers to specific questions about notarization.

The Association is perhaps most widely known as the preeminent publisher of information for and about Notaries. NNA works include:

• *The National Notary*, a magazine for National Notary Association members featuring how-to articles with practical tips on notarizing.

• *Notary Bulletins*, keeping NNA members up to date on developments affecting Notaries, especially new state laws and regulations.

• *Notary Basics Made Easy*, a first-of-its-kind video instruction program that simplifies Notary practices and procedures.

• *Notary Home Study Course*, a work-at-your-own-speed course covering every facet of notarization.

• *Sorry, No Can Do!* and *Sorry, No Can Do! 2*, two volumes that help Notaries explain to customers why some requests for notarizations are improper and cannot be accommodated.

• *Notary Seal & Certificate Verification Manual*, invaluable for any person relying on the authenticity and correctness of legal documents.

• *Notary Public Practices & Glossary*, widely hailed as the Notary's bible, a definitive reference book on notarial procedures.

• State *Notary Law Primers*, explaining a state's notarial statutes in easy-to-understand language.

• The *Model Notary Act*, prototype legislation conceived in 1973 and updated in 1984 by an NNA-recruited panel of secretaries of state, legislators and attorneys, and regularly used by state legislatures in revising their notarial laws.

• *Notary Law & Practice: Cases & Materials*, the definitive and one-of-a-kind text for teaching Notary law to law students in schools and to attorneys in Minimum Continuing Education Seminars (MCLE) seminars, discussing every major judicial decision affecting the Notary's duties.

• Public-service pamphlets informing the general public about the function of a Notary, including *What Is A Notary Public?*, printed in both English and Spanish.

In addition, the National Notary Association offers the highest quality professional supplies, including official seals and stamps, embossers, recordkeeping journals, affidavit stamps, thumbprinting devices and notarial certificates.

Though dedicated primarily to educating and assisting Notaries, the National Notary Association devotes part of its resources to helping lawmakers draft effective notarial statutes and to informing the public about the Notary's vital role in modern society. ■

Index

Page numbers listed in **bold** indicate where the most complete information on a subject can be found. *Italics* indicate the pages where the statutes pertaining to a subject are located.

B

C

Page numbers listed in **bold** indicate where the most complete information on a subject can be found. *Italics* indicate the pages where the statutes pertaining to a subject are located.

Page numbers listed in **bold** indicate where the most complete information on a subject can be found. *Italics* indicate the pages where the statutes pertaining to a subject are located.

Because you can't know everything...

You Should Belong to the National Notary Association

It doesn't matter whether you're a long-time Notary, or a newcomer. Whether you notarize dozens of documents each week, or a few a month.

As a Notary, you should belong to the National Notary Association.

We're a professional association with over 150,000 members from every state and U.S. jurisdiction. And we've devoted our efforts to your needs and concerns for over four decades.

There are many reasons to be a part of the NNA. Among them:

- Notary Information Service — If you have a problem or a question, you can take advantage of our "hotline," fax service, e-mail or mail system for an answer or solution.

- Monthly Publications — THE NATIONAL NOTARY magazine and the NOTARY BULLETIN newspaper will give you informative articles, how-to features, important news stories and helpful tips every month.

- Discounted Supplies and Services — Special member savings on Notary services and supplies, many that are exclusively from the NNA, await you.

With these services and so much more, we're here for you when you need us. You should belong to the National Notary Association.

National Notary Association
Dedicated to Serving Notaries
9350 De Soto Ave., P.O. Box 2402
Chatsworth, CA 91313-2402
Telephone: 1-800-US NOTARY (1-800-876-6827)
Fax: 1-800-833-1211
www.nationalnotary.org

Other Resources from the National Notary Association

'Notary Law & Practice: Cases & Materials'

...The definitive legal text on notarization. Authored by five noted law school professors, *Notary Law & Practice* presents scores of notarization-related court decisions and details how these cases affect you today. You get extensive judicial opinions and commentary about notarizations and related frauds. Hardcover, 6¼" x 9¼", 629 pages.

No. 5100 . . . . $49.95 NNA members / $68.00 non-NNA members

'Notary Home Study Course'

...Step-by-step, illustrated instructions for all the notarial acts you'll likely perform. You'll learn how to complete the many certificates you'll see, notarize unusual documents, avoid common pitfalls, and prevent personal liability. Learn time-saving shortcuts you can take...and can't take. The *Notary Home Study Course* will make your duties as a Notary much, much easier! Softcover, 8¼" x 10¾", 432 pages.

No. 5001 . . . . $34.95 NNA members / $48.00 non-NNA members

'Notary Seal & Certificate Verification Manual'

...Essential for legal and business professionals and government officials who receive or send documents out-of-state. At a glance, the *Notary Seal & Certificate Verification Manual* gives you detailed notarization rules and procedures for all 50 states, the District of Columbia, and five U.S. jurisdictions. Softcover, 8¼" x 10¾", 406 pages.

No. 5143 . . . . $44.95 NNA members / $79.00 non-NNA members

'Notary Basics Made Easy' Video Instruction Program

...Makes reviewing Notary basics as easy as watching TV. From checking signer's identification to affixing your signature and seal, *Notary Basics Made Easy* gives you the know-how you need to begin or enhance your career as a Notary. Complete set includes three VHS video tapes and a handy 16-page Program Guide. Approximate running time: 55 minutes.

No. 5009 . . . . $29.95 NNA members / $50.00 non-NNA members

'State Notary Law Primers'

...Detailed instructions on Notary laws and regulations in the following states:

Arizona ....No. 5130	Missouri ....No. 5122	No. Carolina.......No. 5129
California ....No. 5120	Nevada.................No. 5134	Oregon.................No. 5128
Florida................No. 5121	New Jersey...........No. 5131	Texas ....No. 5123
Hawaii ....No. 5132	New York.............No. 5125	Washington ....No. 5124
Michigan ....No. 5135	*(More states in production.)*	

Softcover, 96 to 148 pages, 5¼" x 8⅜" . . . . . . $12.95 NNA members / $16.00 non-NNA members

---

 National Notary Association
To order, use the form on the back of the opposite page, or call 1-800-876-6827.

'101 Useful Notary Tips'

...Tips on every subject, from acknowledgments and apostilles...to jurats and journals...to seals and signatures make this a perfect, quick reference guide. Softcover, 5½" x 8¼", 46 pages.

No. 5119 . . . . $8.95 NNA members / $14.00 non-NNA members

'12 Steps to a Flawless Notarization'

...Explains how to perform a problem-free notarization, including screening identification, scanning a document and filling out notarial wording. Softcover, 5¼" x 8¼", 48 pages.

No. 5144 . . . . $8.95 NNA members / $14.00 non-NNA members

'ID Checking Guide'

...Pictures and specifications for each state's driver's license, descriptions of non-driver, military and immigration IDs, and credit cards. Drivers License Guide Co., softcover, 6" x 9", 96 pages.

No. 5599. . . . . $17.95 NNA members / $20.00 non-NNA members

'How to Fingerprint'

...Shows you all the steps for taking clear, useable fingerprints for employment, for a special office or for identification of minors. Softcover, 5¼" x 8¼", 110 pages.

No. 5102. . . . . $12.95 NNA members / $18.00 non-NNA members

'How to Take a Notary Journal Thumbprint'

...Explains how a journal thumbprint protects the Notary, document signers and the public. Provides details on how to obtain clear, useable prints. Softcover, 5¼" x 8¼", 64 pages.

No. 5140 . . . . $8.95 NNA members / $14.00 non-NNA members

'Notary Practices & Glossary'

...Covers every important facet of the Notary Public office and provides definitive explanations of notarial procedures. Hardcover, 5½" x 8¾", 200 pages.

No. 5110. . . . . $15.95 NNA members / $22.00 non-NNA members

'Preparing for the California Notary Public Exam'

...Helps you get ready for and pass the exam by explaining California's stringent Notary laws and focusing on what is important for the exam. Softcover, 5¼" x 8¼", 96 pages.

No. 2000. . . . . $12.95 NNA members / $18.00 non-NNA members

'Sorry, No Can Do!' & 'Sorry, No Can Do! 2'

...Easy-to-understand responses to the most common requests for improper notarizations. When asked to preform an improper act, you can show your signer the relevant page and they'll see why you have to turn down the request. Hardcover, 5¼" x 8¼", spiral bound to lay flat.

2 Volume Set, No. 5386 . . . . $21.95 NNA members / $30.00 non-NNA members

Order Form

Membership Information

☐ YES! I want to receive the benefits of membership in the National Notary Association!
Please enroll me as a member for the following term:

☐ 1 Year $34   ☐ 3 Years $79 saves you $23.00!   ☐ 5 Years $119 saves you $51.00!
☐ 2 Years $59 saves you $9.00! ☐ 4 Years $99 saves you $37.00!

Please include your membership dues in total below. There is no tax or shipping charge on your NNA membership.

Item #	Quantity	Description	Price	TOTAL

SHIPPING

Total Order Amount	U.S. Mail/ Standard UPS
UNDER $15	$3.85
$15.01 – $35.00	$4.85
$35.01 – $65.00	$5.85
$65.01 – $95.00	$6.85
$95.01+	$7.85

Books Subtotal

Add state and local taxes on subtotal of books for:
AZ, CA, FL, MI, MO, NV, NJ, NY, TX & WA

← *Add Shipping*

Add Membership Dues

TOTAL Enclosed

Shipping/Payment Information

Name _____

Company _____

Address ☐ Company ☐ Home _____

City _____

State _____ Zip _____

Daytime Phone _____

NNA Member Number (Required for member prices) _____

☐ Check Enclosed — Payable to: National Notary Association

☐ Visa ☐ MasterCard ☐ American Express ☐ Discover

Card Number _____

Card Expires _____

Signature _____

Sorry, but we cannot accept purchase orders to bill on account.

National Notary Association
Dedicated to Serving Notaries

Four Easy Ways to Order:

By Phone:
☎ 1-800-876-6827
(1-800-US NOTARY)
With credit card order

By FAX:
1-800-833-1211
24 hours with credit card order

By Mail:
NNA Notary Supplies Division
9350 De Soto Ave., P.O. Box 2402
Chatsworth, CA 91313-2402

By Internet:
www.nationalnotary.org
With credit card order

Office use only.

When calling refer to
Service Code: A15660